Oracle Certification Prep

Study Guide for

1Z0-052: Oracle Database 11g:

Administration I

Matthew Morris

Study Guide for Oracle Database 11g: Administration I (Exam 1Z0-052) Rev 1.3

Special thanks to Yasir Arsanukaev for proofreading this guide and locating an embarrassingly large number of typos.

ISBN-13: 978-1477565872
ISBN-10: 1477565876

Table of Contents

What to Expect from the Test

The test consists of 70 multiple choice and multiple answer questions. The passing score listed on Oracle Education at this time is 66%, but as with all Oracle certification tests, they note it is subject to change. For multiple-answer questions, you must provide all of the correct answers to get credit for the question. Answer every question on the exam – an unanswered question counts off the same amount as an incorrect one. Take your time reading the question and all of the answers. Sometimes later questions will answer earlier ones and I have found that marking questions I'm not sure of and re-reading them again at the end of the test is valuable.

The number of topics on this test is comparable to other Oracle certification tests. However, the range of topics is not. The Administration I test covers an extremely broad range of topics. Most of the Oracle certification tests have a reasonably narrow focus. The SQL Fundamentals exam covers only SQL; the performance tuning exam covers only tuning topics; and so forth. Because this test covers so many subjects, you should spend extra time preparing for it.

What to Expect from this Study Guide

This document is built around the subject matter topics that Oracle Education has indicated will be tested. I've gathered together material from several Oracle documentation sources along with examples and illustrations to familiarize you with the types of questions you're likely to see on the test. The guide covers a significant percentage of the information and operations that you must be familiar with in order to pass the test.

What this guide is intended to do is to present the information that will be covered on the exam at the level it will likely be asked. The guide assumes that you have at least a rudimentary knowledge of the Oracle database. While the guide works from basic principles of Oracle administration, no book in and of itself is a substitute for hands-on experience. You should install and configure an Oracle database, create users and tables, and practice the concepts discussed on this guide prior to scheduling your exam. Since Oracle has made the Oracle XE version of its database free to download and use, there is no reason why anyone who wants to learn to use Oracle cannot get hands-on experience.

The goal of this guide is to present to you the concepts and information most likely to be the subject of test questions, and to do so in a very compact format that will allow you to read through it more than once to reinforce the information. If much of the information presented in this guide is completely new to you then you need to supplement this guide with other source of study materials to build a firm foundation of Oracle database administration fundamentals. If you have a reasonable grounding in the basic concepts and are comfortable with basic administration tasks, then this book will supply you with the facts you need to pass the exam and improve your skills as a database administrator. If you don't have any experience with Oracle at all, the compressed format of this guide is not likely to be the best method for learning. It might provide you with sufficient information to pass the test, but you're likely to have deficiencies as a database administrator.

If you are new to Oracle and are using this certification as a means to enter the field, then I recommend that you use more than one source of study materials. It is very important that you know this information not just so that you can pass the test, but so that you can do the work of a database administrator. If you have never read the Oracle Concepts manual, I highly recommend doing so. It can be downloaded for free from the Web and it's designed to provide a solid foundation on how the various parts of Oracle function. Likewise the Oracle Database Administrator's Guide is an excellent resource that can be obtained for free. This guide was developed from information in those two manuals, plus about six others from the Oracle documentation library.

Additional Study Resources

The companion website to this series is www.oraclecertificationprep.com.
The site contains many additional resources that can be used to study for
this exam (and others). From the entry page of the website, click on the
'Exams' button, and then select the link for this test. The Exam Details
page contains links to the following information sources:

- Applicable Oracle documentation.
- Third-party books relevant to the exam.
- White papers and articles on Oracle Learning Library on topics
  covered in the exam.
- Articles on the Web that may be useful for the exam.

The website will never link to unauthorized content such as brain dumps
or illegal content such as copyrighted material made available without the
consent of the author. I cannot guarantee the accuracy of the content
links. While I have located the data and scanned it to ensure that it is
relevant to the given exam, I did not write it and have not proofread it
from a technical standpoint. The material on the Oracle Learning Library
is almost certain to be completely accurate and most of the other links
come from highly popular Oracle support websites and are created by
experienced Oracle professionals.

I recommend that you use more than one source of study materials
whenever you are preparing for a certification. Reading information
presented from multiple different viewpoints can help to give you a more
complete picture of any given topic. The links on the website can help
you to do this. Fully understanding the information covered in this
certification is not just valuable so that getting a passing score is more
likely – it will also help you in your career. I guarantee that in the long
run, any knowledge you gain while studying for this certification will
provide more benefit to you than any piece of paper or line on your
resume.

Exploring the Oracle Database Architecture

Gaining a firm understanding the architecture of the Oracle database is key to being able to administer it effectively. Everything that happens, both good and bad, is easier to understand and replicate (or repair) if you know what is going on behind the scenes. An analogy would be operating a car. You can drive a car without having any idea of how an engine functions. However, if you are going to be in charge of maintaining a car, you need to understand at least the basics of how an internal combustion engine works, the importance of changing the oil, keeping belts tight and fluids topped up, etc. The administrator of an Oracle database is the person responsible for maintaining it. This section contains information critical to your ability to do that job well.

The Oracle Relational Database Management System (RDBMS) is an immensely capable (and complex) application designed to provide a comprehensive, open, and integrated information management system. It can manage huge amounts of data in a multiuser environment to provide concurrent access to data for thousands of simultaneous users. It provides a high level of data security, excellent performance, and has extremely effective failure recovery capabilities.

Database vs. Instance

An Oracle database server consists of two distinct components: a database and one or more database instances. In general usage, the term Oracle database is often used to refer to both. The definitions of the two are:

- **Database** – A database is a set of files, located on disk, that store data. These files can exist independently of a database instance.
- **Database instance** – An instance is a set of memory structures that manage database files. An Oracle instance consists of a shared memory area and a set of background processes. An instance can exist independently of database files.

In the conventional configuration, there is a single instance and a single database. However, when using Real Application Clusters, there are multiple instances pointing at a single database. The RAC configuration allows for improved scalability, performance, and fault tolerance.

Oracle Data Guard is a configuration where a primary database server is related to one or more standby databases. Standby databases may be physical standbys that are byte-for-byte copies of the primary and are kept current through the application of redo logs from the primary. Alternately they can be logical standbys which are kept synchronized by SQL statements propagated through Oracle Streams.

The illustration below shows the primary components of an Oracle instance.

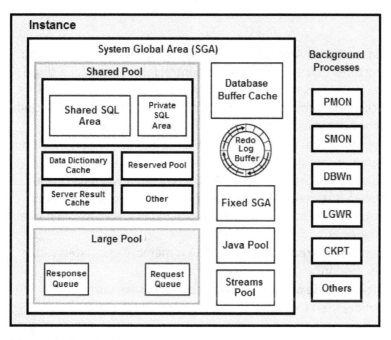

Figure 1: Oracle instance components

A database has physical and logical elements. Physical data consists of what is viewable at the operating system level. For example, database files can be listed using the **ls** command and instance processes can be listed via the Linux **ps** command. Logical data consists of data only viewable from within the database itself. You can query the data dictionary to list the tablespaces that make use of the datafiles in the Operating system, but there is no Linux command that can obtain that information. The logical and physical structures of Oracle are completely separate. Renaming a tablespace does not affect the filenames of the datafiles associated with it and renaming datafiles does not affect the contents of a tablespace.

Explain the Memory Structures

When an Oracle instance is started, background processes are initiated and a memory area is allocated in the operating system. This memory area stores numerous different pieces of information required to run the database. Some of the basic memory structures are:

- **System Global Area (SGA)** – The SGA is a group of shared memory structures that contain data and control information for a single Oracle Database instance. The SGA is shared by all server and background processes. Examples of data stored in the SGA include cached data blocks and shared SQL areas.
- **Program global area (PGA)** – A PGA is a memory region that is not shared. It contains data and control information exclusively for the use of an Oracle process. A PGA is created when an Oracle process is started. One PGA exists for each server process and background process. The collection of individual PGAs is the total instance PGA, or instance PGA.
- **User Global Area (UGA)** – The UGA is memory associated with a user session.
- **Software code areas** – Software code areas are portions of memory used to store code that is being run or can be run.

System Global Area

The SGA is the memory container for all of the data required for the database instance. It consists of numerous memory components. Each component is a pool of memory used to satisfy a particular type of memory allocation request. All except the redo log buffer allocate and deallocate space in units of contiguous memory called granules. You can query the V$SGASTAT view for information about SGA components.

The most important elements of the SGA are:

- **Database Buffer Cache** – The database buffer cache stores copies of data blocks read from data files. A buffer is an address where the buffer manager temporarily caches a currently or recently used data block. All users connected to a database instance share access to the buffer cache. The buffer cache is designed to optimize physical I/O; to keep frequently accessed blocks in the buffer cache; and to write infrequently accessed blocks to disk. It makes use of a Least Recently Used (LRU) algorithm to determine what information should be kept in the buffer cache.
- **Redo Log Buffer** – The redo log buffer is a circular buffer that stores redo entries describing changes made to the database. These entries contain the information required to reconstruct changes made to the database by DML or DDL operations. Database recovery applies redo entries to data files to reconstruct lost changes. The redo entries take up continuous, sequential space in the buffer. The background process log writer (LGWR) writes the redo log buffer to the active online redo log group on disk.
- **Shared Pool** – The shared pool caches various types of program data required by the server. A partial list includes storing parsed SQL, PL/SQL code, system parameters, and data dictionary information. It is involved in almost every operation that occurs in the database. Among other things, every SQL statement issued by users requires an access of the shared pool.
- **Large Pool** – The large pool is an optional memory area in the SGA. It is intended for memory allocations that are larger than is appropriate to store in the shared pool. Examples of this are the UGA for the shared server and the Oracle XA interface and buffers for Recovery Manager (RMAN) I/O slaves.
- **Java Pool** – The Java pool stores all session-specific Java code and data within the Java Virtual Machine (JVM). This includes Java objects that are migrated to the Java session space at end-of-call.
- **Streams Pool** – The Streams pool is used exclusively by Oracle Streams. It stores buffered queue messages and provides memory for Streams capture and apply processes. Unless configured otherwise, the size of the Streams pool starts at zero and grows dynamically as required by Oracle Streams.

- **Fixed SGA** – The fixed SGA is an internal housekeeping area. Among other things, it contains general information required by the background processes about the state of the database and the instance. The size of the fixed SGA is set by the Oracle Database and cannot be altered manually.

Memory Management

Memory management is the process of maintaining optimal sizes for the Oracle instance memory structures. Ideally the size of the memory structures will change as demands on the database change. Initialization parameter settings determine how Oracle manages SGA and instance PGA memory. Oracle allocates and deallocates SGA space in units called granules, which can be 4M, 8M, or 16M in size depending on the OS.

- **Automatic Memory Management** – When using automatic memory management, Oracle manages the SGA and instance PGA memory automatically. This is the simplest method for managing memory and is strongly recommended by Oracle. For databases created with DBCA using the basic installation option, automatic memory management is enabled by default.
- **Automatic Shared Memory Management** – Automatic shared memory management enables you to exercise more control over the size of the SGA and is the default when automatic memory management is disabled. Oracle will tune the total SGA to a supplied target size and will also tune the sizes of SGA components. If you are using a server parameter file, Oracle remembers the sizes of the automatically tuned components across instance shutdowns.
- **Manual Shared Memory Management** – With Manual Shared Memory Management, you set the sizes of several individual SGA components and manually tune individual SGA components. This option provides complete control of individual SGA component sizes.

Memory Management of the Instance PGA

If automatic memory management is not enabled, then the following modes are possible for management of PGA memory:

- **Automatic PGA memory management** – If the PGA_AGGREGATE_TARGET initialization parameter is set to a nonzero value, the database uses automatic PGA memory management. In this mode, the database then tunes the size of the instance PGA to the supplied parameter value and dynamically tunes the sizes of individual PGAs. If PGA_AGGREGATE_TARGET is not explicitly set, then Oracle automatically configures a reasonable default.
- **Manual PGA memory management** – If AMM is not enabled and PGA_AGGREGATE_TARGET is explicitly set to 0, the database defaults to manual PGA management. Although Oracle Database supports the manual PGA memory management method, Oracle strongly recommends automatic PGA memory management.

Describe the Process Structures

A process is an operating system mechanism that has the ability to run a series of steps. Depending on the operating system, this may be called a job, task, or thread. Used in this context, a thread is equivalent to a process. An Oracle database instance has the following process types:

- **Client processes** – These processes run the software code for an application program or an Oracle tool.
- **Background processes** – Background processes consolidate functions that otherwise would require multiple Oracle Database programs running for each client process. Background processes perform I/O and monitor other Oracle Database processes.
- **Server processes** – Server processes communicate with client processes and interact with the database to fulfill requests.

Client Processes

When a user runs a program such as SQL*Developer or SQL*Plus, a client process (also known as a user process) is created by the operating system. Client processes interact with server processes in order to interface with the database. Server processes always run on the same machine as the Oracle database, while client processes generally run on a different machine. The client process has no direct access to the SGA of the database, but the servicing server process does. When the client process runs on the client machine, it is known as two-tier architecture. In some cases, the client process may run on an application server. This is known as a three-tiered architecture.

Connections vs. Sessions

Client processes must communicate with the Oracle server in order to access database information. This is done through the use of connections and sessions. The two are related, but not interchangeable.

- **Connection** – A physical communication pathway between a client process and a database instance. This pathway is created using network software or interprocess communication mechanisms. In general, a connection occurs between a client process and either a server process or a dispatcher.
- **Session** – A logical entity in the database instance that represents the state of a current user login to a database. After a user establishes a connection to a database and authenticates to a database account via a username and password, a session is established for the user. The session lasts until the user disconnects or exits the connecting application.

A single connection can generate multiple sessions. For example SQL*Developer can open multiple sessions concurrently to a given database while only requiring a single connection. A single user account can have multiple sessions open concurrently. All sessions, even those for the same user, are completely independent. The results of uncommitted transactions in one session aren't visible to another session, and issuing a commit in one session does not affect uncommitted transactions in another.

Server Processes

Server processes are created by the Oracle Database to handle the requests of client processes connected to the instance. A client process cannot communicate with the database on its own. It always communicates with the database through a separate server process. Server processes can perform the following tasks:

- Parse and run SQL statements
- Execute PL/SQL code
- Read data blocks from data files into the database buffer cache
- Return results from the database to the application

Oracle server processes can be dedicated or shared.

Dedicated Server Processes

- One client connection is associated with one server process
- The client process communicates directly with its server process
- This server process is dedicated to its client process for the duration of the session
- The server process stores process-specific information and the UGA in its PGA

Shared Server Processes

- Client applications connect to a shared dispatcher process
- The client process communicates directly with its dispatcher process
- The server processes are shared among all of the dispatcher processes
- Each shared server process has its own PGA, but not UGA.
- The UGA for a session is stored in the SGA so that any shared server can access session data

Mandatory Background Processes

The mandatory background processes are present in all typical database configurations. These processes run by default in a database instance started with a minimally configured initialization parameter file. Any processes that contain one or more n's can have multiple incarnations. Each version will be given successive integers (DBW0, DBW1, etc).

- **Process Monitor Process (PMON)** – As its name suggests, PMON monitors all of the other background processes. When a server or dispatcher process terminates abnormally, PMON performs process recovery. It is also responsible for cleaning up the database buffer cache and freeing resources that were allocated for client processes. PMON also registers information about the instance and dispatcher processes with the Oracle Net Listener.
- **System Monitor Process (SMON)** – SMON is in charge of a variety of system-level cleanup duties. The duties assigned to SMON include: performing instance recovery at instance startup if necessary; recovering any terminated transactions that were skipped during instance recovery; cleaning up unused temporary segments; and coalescing contiguous free extents within dictionary-managed tablespaces.
- **Database Writer Process (DBWn)** – DBWn processes write modified buffers in the database buffer cache to disk. All databases have at least one database writer process (DBW0). It's possible to configure additional DBWn processes to improve performance in databases with high levels of data modification. DBWn writes out to datafiles at the following times:

  - ✓ There are no free buffers.
  - ✓ Every 3 seconds
  - ✓ During a checkpoint
  - ✓ When there are too many dirty buffers
  - ✓ When the instance shuts down cleanly
  - ✓ When a tablespace changes status (i.e. is made read-only, or taken offline)
- **Log Writer Process (LGWR)** – LGWR manages the redo log buffer. LGWR writes one contiguous portion of the buffer to the online redo log. The redo log buffer is circular. Once LGWR writes entries from the buffer to an online redo log file, server processes can

copy new entries over the entries that were just written to disk. LGWR will write all redo entries that have been copied into the buffer since the last time it wrote if any of the following are true:

- ✓ A user commits a transaction
- ✓ An online redo log switch occurs
- ✓ Three seconds have passed since LGWR last wrote
- ✓ The redo log buffer is one-third full or contains 1 MB of buffered data
- ✓ DBWn must write modified buffers to disk.

- **Checkpoint Process (CKPT)** – CKPT updates the control file and data file headers with checkpoint information and signals DBWn to write blocks to disk. Checkpoint information includes the checkpoint position, SCN, location in online redo log to begin recovery, and other data useful to recovery operations. CKPT performs full checkpoints only at database shutdown or on request.
- **Manageability Monitor Processes (MMON and MMNL)** – MMON performs many tasks related to the Automatic Workload Repository (AWR). For example, MMON reports when a metric violates its threshold value, takes snapshots, and captures statistics value for recently modified SQL objects. The manageability monitor lite process (MMNL) writes statistics from the Active Session History (ASH) buffer in the SGA to disk.
- **Recoverer Process (RECO)** – In a distributed database, RECO resolves failures in distributed transactions. The RECO process of a node automatically connects to other databases involved in an in-doubt distributed transaction. When a connection is reestablished, RECO automatically resolves all in-doubt transactions.

Optional Background Processes

An optional background process is any background process not defined as mandatory. The majority of optional background processes are specific to tasks or features.

- **Archiver Processes (ARCn)** – ARCn copies online redo log files to offline storage after a redo log switch occurs. The ARCn processes can also collect transaction redo data and transmit it to standby databases. ARCn processes exist only when the database is in ARCHIVELOG mode and automatic archiving is enabled.

- **Job Queue Processes (CJQ0 and Jnnn)** – Job queue processes are used to run user jobs, often in batch mode. A job is a user-defined task scheduled to run one or more times. The job coordinator process (CJQ0) is automatically started and stopped as needed by Oracle. The coordinator process dynamically spawns job queue slave processes (Jnnn) to run the jobs.
- **Flashback Data Archiver Process (FBDA)** – FBDA archives historical rows of tracked tables into Flashback Data Archives. Any time a DML transaction on a tracked table commits, FBDA stores the pre-image of the rows into the Flashback Data Archive. It also keeps metadata on the current rows.
- **Space Management Coordinator Process (SMCO)** – SMCO coordinates the execution of space management tasks, such as proactive space allocation and space reclamation. SMCO dynamically spawns slave processes (Wnnn) to implement tasks.

Overview of Storage Structures

The primary purpose of the Oracle RDBMS is to store data. This task is accomplished through the use of physical and logical storage structures.

Physical Storage Structures

The physical database structures are the operating system files used to store the data. At the time a database is created, the following files are created:

- **Data files** – Physical data files contain all the data of the database. All logical database structures, such as tables and indexes, are physically stored in data files.
- **Control files** – Control files contains information specifying the physical structure of the database, including the database name and the names and locations of the database files. It also tracks database wide synchronization through the use of System Change Numbers (SCNs). A common SCN between the control files and all datafile headers indicates the database is consistent. Control files

are multiplexed, in that Oracle maintains multiple identical copies for redundancy.

- **Online redo log files** – A set of two or more online redo log files makes up an online redo log. An online redo log contains redo entries which record all changes made to data in the database. The redo log entries can be used to redo changes made to the database in the event of an instance failure. There are always two or more redo log groups in a database. When one group has been filled, LGWR points to the next log group. This is called a log switch and will cause a thread checkpoint to occur. In a thread checkpoint, the database writes to disk all buffers modified by redo in a specific thread before a certain target. Like control files, redo log files are multiplexed for redundancy.

There are several other files that are important for an Oracle database server, including parameter and diagnostic files. Files that are important for database recovery include backup files and archived redo log files.

Logical Storage Structures

Logical storage structures enable Oracle Database to have fine-grained control over disk space usage. The following lists the logical structures Oracle uses, from smallest to largest.

- **Data blocks** – At the finest level of granularity, data is stored in data blocks. One data block corresponds to a specific number of bytes on disk.
- **Extents** – An extent is a specific number of logically contiguous data blocks, obtained in a single allocation, and used to store a specific type of information.
- **Segments** – A segment is a set of extents allocated for a user object (for example, a table or index), undo data, or temporary data.
- **Tablespaces** – A database is divided into logical storage units called tablespaces. A tablespace is the logical container for a segment. Each tablespace contains at least one data file. Tablespaces can either be permanent or temporary. Permanent tablespaces hold permanent information, such as tables and indexes. Temporary tablespaces are used for transient operations, such as sorting.

Preparing the Database Environment

Unless you are creating a test or development database that is either non-critical or time limited, taking time to prepare prior to the creation of an Oracle database is essential to your future peace of mind. If you create a database with poor specifications, you may well be creating headaches that will be with you for months or years to come. After you plan your database using the guidelines below, you can create the database with the Database Configuration Assistant (DBCA) or a SQL command. As a general rule, an initial database is created during the Oracle Database software installation. However, it is also possible to create a database after installation.

Pre-Creation Planning Tasks:

- Plan the database tables and indexes and estimate the amount of space they will require.
- Plan the layout of the underlying operating system files.
- Decide on the global database name, which is the name and location of the database within the network structure.
- Familiarize yourself with the initialization parameters contained in the initialization parameter file.
- Select the database character set.
- Consider what time zones your database must support.
- Select the standard database block size. The DB_BLOCK_SIZE parameter cannot be changed after the database is created.
- If the online redo log files will be stored on disks with a 4K byte sector size, determine whether you must manually specify redo log block size.
- Determine the appropriate initial sizing for the SYSAUX tablespace.
- Plan for a default tablespace for non-SYSTEM users to use.
- Plan for the undo tablespace to manage your undo data.
- Develop a backup and recovery strategy to protect the database from failure.

Identify the tools for Administering an Oracle Database

Tasks of a Database Administrator

As identified in the Oracle Database Administrator's Guide, the tasks of an Oracle DBA are:

- **Evaluate the Database Server Hardware** – You need to identify the available computer resources that can be utilized by the database. These resources should include: the number and size of hard disks and tape drives, and the amount of system memory available for use by the database.
- **Install the Oracle Database Software** – A DBA will install the Oracle Database server software and any front-end tools or applications that access the database.
- **Plan the Database** – The DBA must plan the following aspects of the database: the overall design, the logical storage structure, and the backup strategy.
- **Create and Open the Database** – After a database has been designed, the DBA must create the database either through the DBCA tool or the CREATE DATABASE command and open the database for use.
- **Back Up the Database** – Once the base database has been created, the DBA must take an initial backup and schedule future database backups at regular intervals.
- **Enroll System Users** – The DBA must create database users, and grant appropriate privileges and roles to them.
- **Implement the Database Design** – The DBA must implement the planned logical structure database by creating any necessary tablespaces not generated during the database creation and creating required database objects.
- **Tune Database Performance** – Monitoring and optimizing database performance is an ongoing DBA responsibility.
- **Download and Install Patches** – On a regular basis, the DBA should download and install database patches.

Tools & Utilities

Following are some of the products, tools, and utilities that a database administrator can use to configure and control the Oracle Database:

- **Oracle Universal Installer (OUI)** – OUI is a utility that installs your Oracle software and can add or remove optional components. At the end of installation, it can automatically call the Oracle Database Configuration Assistant.
- **Oracle Database Configuration Assistant (DBCA)** – DBCA is a utility that allows you to use predefined templates supplied by Oracle to create a database.
- **Database Upgrade Assistant** – The Database Upgrade Assistant is a tool that assists in upgrading your existing database to a new release.
- **Net Configuration Assistant (NETCA)** – NETCA is a utility for configuring listeners and naming methods in the Oracle Database network.
- **Oracle Net Manager** – Net Manager allows you to configure Oracle Net Services for an Oracle home on a local client or server host. It has the ability to configure naming, naming methods, profiles, and listeners.
- **Oracle Net Configuration Assistant** – Run automatically during software installation, the assistant configures basic network components during installation. These include listener names and protocol addresses, naming methods, net service names in a tnsnames.ora file, and directory server usage.
- **Listener Control Utility** – The Listener Control utility enables you to configure listeners to receive client connections.
- **Oracle Enterprise Manager (OEM)** – OEM is a web-based system management tool that provides centralized management of a database environment.
- **SQL*Plus** – SQL*Plus is an interactive and batch query tool included in every Oracle Database installation. It has a command-line user interface that acts as the client when connecting to the database.
- **SQL*Developer** – Oracle SQL Developer is a free graphical tool that simplifies database development and administration tasks.

Using SQL Developer, users can browse and update database objects, run SQL statements, and edit PL/SQL statements.

- **Recovery Manager (RMAN)** – RMAN is an Oracle Database utility that integrates with an Oracle database to perform backup and recovery activities.
- **SQL*Loader** – SQL*Loader loads data from external files into database tables.
- **Oracle Data Pump** – Data Pump enables high-speed loading and unloading of data and metadata from one database to another.
- **Oracle LogMiner** – Oracle LogMiner enables you to query redo log files through a SQL interface.
- **ADR Command Interpreter (ADRCI)** – ADRCI is a command-line utility that enables you to investigate problems, view health check reports, and package and upload first-failure diagnostic data to Oracle Support.

Plan an Oracle Database installation

As a Database administrator it will be part of your duties to evaluate how the Oracle Database and its applications can best use the available server resources. Your evaluation should answer the following questions:

- How many hard disk drives are available for use by Oracle
- Are any tape drives are available to use in your backup strategy
- How much physical RAM is available for the Oracle database instances

System Requirements

All of the requirements listed are for an Oracle database running under Linux x86-64. Requirements for other operating systems will vary slightly. Refer to the Installation Guide for the appropriate operating system for more details.

Memory Requirements

The memory requirements for installing Oracle Database 11g Release 2 under Linux is 1 GB but 2 or more GB is recommended. The amount of swap space recommended depends on the amount or RAM in the system.

- For systems with 1-2 GB of ram, swap space should be 150% of the RAM.
- For systems with 2-16 GB of ram, swap space should be equal to the RAM.
- For systems with >16 GB of ram, swap space should be 16GB.

Disk Space Requirements

You will require 1GB of space in the /tmp directory before installing Oracle Database 11g Release 2 (11.2) under any version of Linux. If you have less available space than that, you will need to free up space or add additional space to the /tmp mount point. For the Oracle software, you'll need the following minimum amount of space to install the software files and data files:

Enterprise Edition

- 4.35 GB for software files
- 1.7 GB for data files

Standard Edition

- 4.22 GB for software files
- 1.5 GB for data files

In addition to the memory and space requirements, there are several additional requirements that must be considered. These requirements are beyond the scope of the test. You must refer to the appropriate installation guide for details. However, you should be aware that under Linux, the following requirements should be verified before installing Oracle:

- Operating System Requirements
- Kernel Requirements
- Package Requirements
- Compiler Requirements
- Additional Software Requirements

The Oracle installer has a list of checks that it performs prior to starting the software install. It makes the following checks (among others):

- A 64-bit installation is not being installed into a 32-bit home (or the reverse)
- Various operating system parameters are set appropriately
- The OS platform is one that is supported
- The DISPLAY environment variable is set and that the user has X-Windows permissions for it.
- The OS has sufficient swap space.
- The directory being used for the ORACLE_HOME is empty or is a release that can be installed over.
- Any required operating system patches are installed.

Install the Oracle software by using Oracle Universal Installer (OUI)

Optimal Flexible Architecture (OFA)

Oracle's Optimal Flexible Architecture is a set of standardized configuration guidelines. The OFA standard helps to organize database software and configure databases to allow multiple databases, of different versions to coexist. The Optimal Flexible Architecture helps to associate a given ORACLE_BASE with an Automatic Diagnostic Repository (ADR) to store diagnostic data to properly collect incidents. The Oracle Universal Installer will place Oracle Database components in OFA-compliant directory locations, and assign default permissions that follow OFA guidelines. Oracle highly recommends the use of Optimal Flexible Architecture.

To implement all of the OFA recommendations for a database, you must have three file systems located on separate physical drives or make use of a drive array using RAID architecture.

OFA Naming Conventions

File system mount points should use the syntax /pm, where p is a string constant and m is a unique key used to distinguish each mount point. Examples would be /u01 and /u02, or /drive01 and /drive02.

ORACLE_BASE is the top level directory used to install Oracle software products. The same Oracle base directory can be utilized for multiple software installations. However, if multiple OS users install Oracle software on the same system, each user must have their own ORACLE_BASE directory.

In describing the OFA directory naming conventions, the following variables will be used to indicate the logic:

- **pm** – A mount point name
- **s** – A standard directory name
- **u** – The name of the OS user performing the installation
- **d** – database name
- **i** – instance name
- **type** – The type of installation
- **n** – A numeric string
- **v** – The version of the software
- **h** – The ORACLE_BASE directory
- **a** – A standard admin directory name
- **q** – A string (often oradata) to indicate the presence of Oracle data.
- **t** – An Oracle tablespace name

Using the above variables, Oracle base directories should use the syntax /pm/s/u. If an install were made to the u02 mount point by the oracle OS user, with the standard Linux directory name 'app', the ORACLE_BASE directory would be: /u01/app/oracle.

One of the benefits of using the OFA standard is that it allows multiple versions of Oracle software to run concurrently. You should utilize the OFA naming convention when installing product software to assist in this goal. Oracle product software should be installed in a directory matching the pattern /pm/s/u/product/v/type_[n]. An example for an install of Oracle 11G database software might be: /u01/app/oracle/product/11.2.0/dbhome_1.

To facilitate the organization of administrative data, Oracle recommends that database-specific administration files be stored in subdirectories matching the pattern /h/admin/d/a/. The recommended database administration file subdirectory names are:

- **arch** – Archived redo log files
- **adump** – Audit files
- **create** – Contains the Data Pump file dp.log
- **dpdump** – Default directory for Data Pump operations. Scripts used to create the database
- **exp** – Database export files
- **logbook** – Files recording the status and history of the database
- **pfile** – Instance parameter files
- **scripts** – Ad hoc SQL scripts

For example, /u01/app/oracle/admin/orcl/scripts/ is the scripts subdirectory associated with the database named orcl. The bdump, cdump, and udump directories used for dump files in previous releases have been replaced by Automatic Diagnostic Repository (ADR) directories in Oracle 11g. The ADR diagnostic data goes into the /h/diag/rdbms/d/i/ directory.

The OFA also provides a standard for file names in addition to directory paths. The standards below are only for files stored as normal operating system, files. When making use of Oracle Managed Files (OMF) and or Oracle Automatic Storage Management disk groups, a different naming convention is utilized. For more information about these, you should refer to the Oracle Database Administrator's Guide. The following are the recommended file naming conventions for database files:

- **Control files** – /h/q/d/control.ctl
- **Redo log files** – /h/q/d/redon.log
- **Data files** – /h/q/d/tn.dbf

You should never store files other than the ones listed above in the path /h/q/d. This includes control files, redo log files, or database files from other Oracle databases. When the naming convention is utilized properly, it is easy to determine the database to which any given file belongs.

Configuring the OS Environment

There are a number of operating system environment variables that are utilized by Oracle and the Oracle Universal Installer. The OS environment must be properly set prior to running the installer in order for the installation to function correctly. OUI is normally run from the oracle account of the operating system. You must configure the environment of the oracle user prior to initiating the install. Some environment variables must be set, and others are optional, but setting them prior to the install can avoid difficulties later. You should view the appropriate installation guide for the operating system under which you will be performing the install for details on setting environment variables.

Under Linux, the following environment variables must be set:

- The default file mode creation mask (umask) must be set to 022
- The XWindows DISPLAY variable must be set properly.
- The TMP and TMPDIR environment variables must be pointing to the tmp mount point.

The following Oracle environment variables don't have to be set, but ideally should be.

- ORACLE_BASE – sets the base of the directory structure use for OFA.
- ORACLE_SID – Sets the initial instance name used by the OS account.
- ORACLE_HOME – Specifies the directory where the Oracle software is installed.
- NLS_LANG – Specifies language, territory and character set settings.
- LD_LIBRARY_PATH – Specifies the path to Oracle-installed libraries for Linux.

Running the Oracle Universal Installer

For any type of installation process, start Oracle Universal Installer and install the software, as follows:

1. Log in as the OS user that will be the software owner (typically, oracle).
2. Mount the disk containing the installation media if required.
3. To start Oracle Universal Installer, issue the command /directory_path/runInstaller, where directory_path is the path of the database directory on the installation media.
4. Select the product to be installed.
5. Select either the basic or advanced installation.
6. Follow the prompts in the install screens.

If you chose to create a starter database during the installation, OUI will invoke the Oracle Net Configuration Assistant and the Oracle Database Configuration Assistant (DBCA). The Net Configuration Assistance will walk you through the steps to configure the Oracle Listener and naming methods. DBCA is the application that will actually create the starter database.

Creating an Oracle Database

After you plan the structure of your database, you can create it with either a graphical tool or a SQL command. As a general rule, a database is created during the Oracle Database software installation. However, it's also possible to create a database after installation. The creation of an Oracle database prepares several operating system files to work together. The CREATE DATABASE statement is used only once for any given database, regardless of how many datafiles it is made of or how many instances access it.

There are two database configurations that broadly determine the usage to which a database is intended. The first of these two configurations is for data warehouses. The second classification is databases geared toward Online Transaction Processing (OLTP). Some of the qualities of these two are:

- **Data Warehouse** – A relational database designed for query and analysis rather than for transaction processing. Usually contains data derived from historical transaction data. Data tends to be loaded into the warehouse using batch processing rather than individual transactions. The primary non-batch activity against the database is queries – generally against large amounts of data.
- **OLTP** – An OLTP database designed for high numbers of small transactions. It tends to have high amounts of traffic inserting, updating, and deleting data.

The two categories are the endpoints of the spectrum of database usage. Many, if not most, databases fall somewhere in-between the two definitions. However, as a general rule, databases will lean toward one category or the other. The two types require very different tuning characteristics for optimum performance, so identifying which of the two a database leans toward is important from a performance standpoint. The Database Configuration Assistant has templates for creating a database for these two types, plus a third 'General Purpose' database that mixes characteristics of the two.

Create a database by using the Database Configuration Assistant (DBCA)

Oracle's Database Configuration Assistant (DBCA) is a much more automated means of creating a database than using the CREATE DATABASE statement. In addition, once DBCA has completed, the database is immediately ready to use. It's possible for DBCA to be launched by OUI, depending upon the type of install used. DBCA can also be launched as a standalone tool at any point after the Oracle software has been installed.

DBCA has two modes of operation: interactive mode or noninteractive/silent mode. The interactive mode makes use of a graphical user interface and guides you through creating and configuring a database. The noninteractive mode allows you to create the database via a script. DBCA is run in noninteractive mode by specifying command-line arguments, a response file, or both.

Creating a Database with Interactive DBCA

To start DBCA:

Log on to your computer as a member of the group that is authorized to install Oracle and to create and run the database. To start DBCA on UNIX or Linux, or at the command-line prompt in Microsoft Windows, enter the following command: dbca. The dbca executable is located in the ORACLE_HOME/bin directory. Once started, the DBCA user interface guides you through a step-by-step process to create a database.

Creating a Database Using DBCA

- **Operations** – Select Create a Database and click Next to start the guided workflow for creating a database.
- **Database Templates** – Preconfigured or user-created templates allow you to select the type of database to create, with settings optimized for a particular style of workload.
- **Database Identification** – Enter the Global Database Name and the system identifier.
- **Management Options** – Allows you to set up your database so it can be managed with Oracle Enterprise Manager.

- **Database Credentials** – You will specify the passwords for the database administrative accounts.
- **Database File Locations** – You will specify the type of storage and the locations for the Oracle database files. The files might be stored as operating system files, ASM files, or on a Clustered File System.
- **Recovery Configuration** – You will define recovery options such as a fast recovery area and archivelog mode for your database.
- **Database Content** – The database can be created with content using either the sample schemas or custom scripts.
- **Initialization Parameters** – This screen allows you to access windows to change the default initialization parameter settings.
- **Database Storage** – Allows you to verify and/or change the database storage structure.
- **Creation Options** – Allows you create the database, save the settings as a template, or generate database creation scripts.

Creating a Database with Noninteractive/Silent DBCA

The following example creates a database by passing command-line arguments to DBCA:

```
dbca -silent -createDatabase -templateName
    General_Purpose.dbc -gdbname oraprod -sid oraprod -
    responseFile NO_VALUE -characterSet AL32UTF8 -
    memoryPercentage 30 -emConfiguration LOCAL
Enter SYSTEM user password:
password
Enter SYS user password:
password
Copying database files
1% complete
3% complete
. . .
```

It's possible to have a completely silent operation by redirecting **stdout** to a file. However, to do this you must supply passwords for the administrative accounts in command-line arguments or in a response file. You can view all of the DBCA command-line arguments, by running dbca with the parameter -help (dbca -help).

Deleting a Database with DBCA

To delete a database in DBCA, you will execute dbca from a terminal window and click through past the welcome screen. From the Operations screen you can select 'Delete a Database.' You will be given a list of databases. Select the database to be deleted. Click finish and then confirm the deletion when asked by DBCA.

Managing the Oracle Instance

Setting database initialization parameters

When an Oracle instance starts, it makes use of an initialization parameter file to determine many of the database settings that will be used. At minimum, this file must specify the DB_NAME parameter. If the file contains nothing else, all other parameters will be set to default values. There are two types of parameter file that Oracle can use: a text-based parameter file that is read-only to the Oracle instance (PFILE), or a binary file that the instance can both read from and write to (SPFILE). When an instance stats, Oracle uses the following steps to locate an initialization parameter file. It will use the first file it locates:

1. It looks for spfile[SID].ora
2. It looks for spfile.ora
3. It looks for init[SID].ora

The recommended option is to utilize the binary file. It is called a server parameter file or spfile. Unlike the other options, with a spfile, you can change initialization parameters using ALTER SYSTEM commands and have those changes persist across a database shutdown and startup. The spfile also provides a method by which Oracle can self-tune. A spfile can be created manually from your text-based initialization file. Alternately, DBCA can automatically generate one when the database is created. When a server parameter file does not exist, the instance will start using a text initialization parameter file. At startup, the instance initially searches for a server parameter file in a default location. Only if it does not find one will the instance will search for a text initialization parameter file. It's also possible to bypass an existing server parameter file by naming a PFILE as a STARTUP argument.

The default file name for the text initialization parameter file is init[SID].ora. For a database with a SID of oraprod, the default filename would be initoraprod.ora. The default location under Unix and Linux is in the ORACLE_HOME/dbs directory. Under MS Windows, the file would be stored in ORACLE_HOME\database by default.

Many of the database initialization parameters can be dynamically changed using the ALTER SYSTEM statement. For instances using a spfile, such changes can persist across shutdowns. However, if you are using a text initialization parameter file, any changes made via ALTER SYSTEM are effective only for the current instance. You must update them manually in the initialization parameter file to make them permanent.

The text initialization parameter file contains name/value pairs in one of the following forms:

- **Single-Value Parameters** – parameter_name=value
- **Multiple-Value Parameters** – parameter_name=(value[,value] …)

Multiple-value parameters can also be entered on multiple lines using the same format as a single parameter. If a single-value parameter appears on more than one line in the file, only the last value will be used.

Some initialization parameters derive their values from the values of other parameters. As a general rule, the values for derived parameters should not be altered. However, if they are explicitly set, then the specified value will override the calculated value. An example of a derived parameter is SESSIONS. This parameter is calculated from the value of the PROCESSES parameter. Unless SESSIONS is set explicitly, when the value of PROCESSES changes, then the default value of SESSIONS changes as well.

The host operating system will determine the valid values or value ranges of some initialization parameters. The DB_BLOCK_BUFFERS parameter indicates the number of data buffers in main memory. The maximum allowable value for this parameter depends on the operating system. In addition, the size of data block buffers, set by DB_BLOCK_SIZE, defaults to 8K under most operating systems.

Common Initialization Parameters

The following are all commonly set initialization parameters. These and other initialization parameters are listed in more detail in the Oracle 11G Reference Manual.

- **DB_NAME** – Determines the local component of the database name.
- **DB_DOMAIN** – Indicates the domain (logical location) within a network structure. This parameter is optional. The combination of the DB_NAME and DB_DOMAIN must create a database name that is unique within a network.
- **CONTROL_FILES** – Specifies one or more control filenames for the database. Control files are generated at the time a database is created using the names specified by the CONTROL_FILES parameter. If you do not include CONTROL_FILES in the initialization parameter file, Oracle will create a control file in the same directory as the initialization parameter file, using a default operating system–dependent filename.
- **PROCESSES** – Determines the maximum number of OS processes that can connect to Oracle simultaneously. At minimum, this parameter must have a minimum value of one for each background process plus one for each user process.
- **MEMORY_TARGET** – Sets a target memory size for the instance. The total memory used by the instance will remain reasonably constant, based on the supplied value. The instance will automatically distribute memory between the system global area (SGA) and the instance program global area (instance PGA).
- **SGA_TARGET** – If MEMORY_TARGET is not set, you can enable the automatic shared memory management feature by setting the SGA_TARGET parameter to a nonzero value. This parameter sets the total size of the SGA. Oracle will automatically tune the SGA components as needed.
- **SGA_MAX_SIZE** – Specifies the maximum size of the System Global Area for the lifetime of the instance. If you do not specify SGA_MAX_SIZE, then Oracle Database selects a default value that is the sum of all components specified or defaulted at the time of initialization.
- **PGA_AGGREGATE_TARGET** – Allows you to control the total amount of memory dedicated to the instance PGA.
- **UNDO_MANAGEMENT** – When set to AUTO or null, this parameter enables automatic undo management. When set to MANUAL, undo management will use manual mode.
- **UNDO_TABLESPACE** – This parameter is optional, and valid only in automatic undo management mode. The parameter specifies

the name of an undo tablespace. It is used only when the database has multiple undo tablespaces.

- **DB_BLOCK_SIZE** – Sets the standard block size for the database. The standard block size is used for the SYSTEM tablespace and will be used for other tablespaces by default. Oracle can support up to four additional nonstandard block sizes.
- **COMPATIBLE** – Used to make Oracle act as if it were an earlier release of the software.
- **DIAGNOSTIC_DEST** – Used to determine the location of the Automatic Diagnostic Repository.
- **LOG_ARCHIVE_DEST_n** – Determines where to write Archived Redo Logs.
- **OPEN_CURSORS** – Sets the maximum number of open cursors for an individual session.
- **SESSIONS** – Sets the maximum number of sessions that can connect to the database.

Displaying Database Parameters

You can determine the values of instance parameters in from either SQL*Plus or SQL Developer. Parameter values can be determined by querying the V$PARAMETER view:

```
SELECT name, value
FROM   v$parameter
WHERE  name LIKE '%size%';

NAME                           VALUE
-----------------------------  --------
sga_max_size                   1073741824
shared_pool_size               0
large_pool_size                0
java_pool_size                 0
streams_pool_size              0
shared_pool_reserved_size      18454937
java_max_sessionspace_size     0
db_block_size                  8192
```

You can also use the "show parameter" command to display one or more parameters. The parameter name given in the command is treated as a wildcard. Any parameters for which the supplied value is a part of the name will be displayed:

```
show parameter pool_size

NAME                              TYPE        VALUE
-------------- ------ -----
global_context_pool_size          string
java_pool_size                    big integer 0
large_pool_size                   big integer 0
olap_page_pool_size               big integer 0
shared_pool_size                  big integer 0
streams_pool_size                 big integer 0
```

If you give a complete parameter name, only the one parameter will be returned:

```
show parameter large_pool_size

NAME                              TYPE        VALUE
-------------- ------ -----
large_pool_size                   big integer 0
```

You can use the "show spparameter" command to view parameter values that have been specified in the server parameter file. Since there is nothing in the value column below, the parameter value has not been specified in the file:

```
show spparameter shared_pool_reserved_size

SID   NAME                        TYPE        VALUE
--- -------------- ------ ------
*       shared_pool_reserved_size  big integer
```

The following database views can be used to locate information about database parameters.

- **V$PARAMETER** – Displays the values of initialization parameters in effect for the current session.
- **V$PARAMETER2** – Similar to V$PARAMETER. However it is easier to distinguish list parameter values in this view because each list parameter value appears in a separate row.
- **V$SYSTEM_PARAMETER** – Displays the values of initialization parameters in effect for the instance.
- **V$SPPARAMETER** – Displays the current contents of the SPFILE. It returns FALSE values in the ISSPECIFIED column if an SPFILE is not being used by the instance.

Altering Initialization Parameter Values

There are two broad classes of initialization parameters: static and dynamic. Static parameters affect the entire database and can only be modified by changing the PFILE or SPFILE and require a database shutdown before they will take effect. Dynamic parameters can be altered while the instance is running and will take effect without requiring a shutdown. Dynamic parameters can be further subdivided into session and system-level parameters:

- **Session-level parameters** – Affect only a single session. These can be altered using the ALTER SESSION command and will only affect the session in which that command is executed. The changed values expire as soon as that session is closed.
- **System-level parameters** – Affect the entire database and all sessions. They can be set with the ALTER SYSTEM command and can either be temporary or permanent.

You can use the ALTER SYSTEM statement with the SET clause to alter initialization parameter values. When doing so, there is a second optional SCOPE clause that determines the scope of the change. For instances that are not using a server parameter file, only the SCOPE=MEMORY is a valid option. Permanent parameter changes will have to be made by manually altering the text-based parameter file.

- **SCOPE = SPFILE** – The change is applied in the server parameter file only. No change is made to the current instance. The change is effective at the next startup and is persistent. This scope can be used with either static or dynamic parameters.
- **SCOPE = MEMORY** – The change is applied in memory only. The change is made to the current instance and is effective immediately. The change is not persistent because the server parameter file is not updated. This scope is only valid for dynamic parameters.
- **SCOPE = BOTH** – The change is applied in both the server parameter file and memory. The change is made to the current instance and is effective immediately. The effect is persistent because the server parameter file is updated. This scope is only valid for dynamic parameters.

There are two more optional modifiers that add additional functionality to the ALTER SYSTEM command:

- **COMMENT** – For instances using a server parameter file, this clause can be used with the SPFILE and BOTH options to add a comment to the SPFILE along with the changed parameter (i.e. 'Changed on 4/28/2012 by Matt Morris').
- **DEFERRED** – This keyword is valid for dynamic parameters with the MEMORY and BOTH options for parameters that are session-specific. The change will be made effective only for future sessions.

Describe the stages of database startup and shutdown

Starting a Database

Starting a database creates the memory portion of the Oracle server – the database instance. Also as part of the startup, you determine the state of the database. The normal procedure for starting a database performs three steps: First the instance is created; second the database is mounted; and third the database is opened. When all three are performed, the Oracle database becomes available for any valid user to connect and access data.

There are several methods that can be used to start up a database instance:

- **SQL*Plus** – From a SQL*Plus session, connect to Oracle Database with administrator privileges, and then issue the STARTUP command.
- **Recovery Manager** – From within the RMAN interface, you can execute STARTUP and SHUTDOWN commands.
- **Oracle Enterprise Manager** – OEM has several tools to assist in administering a database, including the ability to perform startup and shutdown.
- **SRVCTL** – If Oracle Restart is installed and configured for your database, SRVCTL is the only recommended method to start the database.

When issuing a startup from SQL*Plus, there are several options to determine the state and availability of the database:

- **STARTUP NOMOUNT** – Start the instance without mounting a database. This does not allow access to the database and usually would be done only for database creation or the re-creation of control files.
- **STARTUP MOUNT** – Start the instance and mount the database, but leave it closed. This state allows for certain DBA activities, but does not allow general access to the database.
- **STARTUP OPEN** – Start the instance, and mount and open the database in unrestricted mode, allowing access to all users. This is the default method for starting a database.
- **STARTUP RESTRICT** – Start the instance, and mount and open the database in restricted mode, allowing access for database administrators only.
- **STARTUP FORCE** – Force the instance to start after a startup or shutdown problem by issuing a SHUTDWN ABORT and then a STARTUP NORMAL.
- **STARTUP OPEN RECOVER** – Start the instance and have complete media recovery begin immediately.

Shutting Down a Database

An Oracle instance can be shut down using SQL*Plus by connecting as SYSOPER or SYSDBA and issuing the SHUTDOWN command. For databases managed by Oracle Restart, the srvctl stop database command is the only recommended way to shut down the database. When shutting down a database, there are several different modes to choose from: normal, immediate, transactional, and abort. The difference in the modes is that each waits for certain events to occur before executing the shutdown. There is a one-hour timeout period for these events.

Shutdown Normal

The SQL*Plus SHUTDOWN has a NORMAL clause, but this is optional because normal is the default shutdown method. After a normal shutdown, the database will not require any instance recovery procedure on the next startups. Normal database shutdown proceeds as follows:

- No new connections are allowed after the shutdown is issued.
- The database waits for all currently connected users to disconnect from the database before shutting down.

Shutdown Immediate

To shutdown a database in the immediate mode, issue SHUTDOWN IMMEDIATE from SQL*Plus while connected with the SYSDBA or SYSOPER privilege. The immediate database shutdown is used when the database must be taken down while unattended, or if there is an urgent need to have it down in a short timeframe. After a normal shutdown, the database will not require any instance recovery procedure on the next startup. Immediate database shutdown proceeds as follows:

- Neither new connections, nor new transactions are allowed after the statement is issued.
- Uncommitted transactions are rolled back. If there are long running transactions underway, this method of shutdown might not complete quickly.
- Users currently connected without running transactions are disconnected after rolling back any completed (but uncommitted) transactions.

Shutdown Transactional

To shutdown a database in the transactional mode, issue SHUTDOWN TRANSACTIONAL from SQL*Plus while connected with the SYSDBA or SYSOPER privilege. This mode allows you to perform a planned shutdown of an instance while allowing active transactions to complete first. Shutdown Transaction MAY take longer than a shutdown immediate because transactions in progress at the time the shutdown is initiated don't just have to finish running, but must be committed (or rolled back) as well. It could conceivably be shorter, however. If a million-row update is in process when a SHUTDOWN IMMEDIATE is issued, the DML must run to completion, but will then be rolled back automatically. The same statement with SHUTDOWN transactional must complete, but if committed at completion will end the transaction and allow the database to shutdown. A commit is much faster than a rollback. The next startup of the database will not require any instance recovery procedures. A transactional shutdown prevents clients from losing work. A transactional database shutdown proceeds as follows

- Neither new connections, nor new transactions are allowed after the statement is issued.
- Once all transactions have completed, client sessions to the instance are disconnected.
- After all client sessions are disconnected, the instance shuts down.

Shutdown Abort

To shutdown a database in the abort mode, issue SHUTDOWN ABORT from SQL*Plus while connected with the SYSDBA or SYSOPER privilege. Issuing a shutdown abort will shut down a database instance nearly instantaneously. Shutdown aborts should be avoided if at all possible. You should perform this type of shutdown only when there is a need to shut down the database immediately, or the database is behaving erratically and the other shutdown methods are not working. The next startup of the database will require automatic instance recovery procedures. An aborted database shutdown proceeds as follows:

- Neither new connections, nor new transactions are allowed after the statement is issued.
- Current client SQL statements being processed by Oracle are immediately terminated.
- Uncommitted transactions are not rolled back.
- Oracle implicitly disconnects all connected users.

The actions performed for each of the shutdown options is summarized in the table below:

Shutdown Option	N	T	I	A
New connections allowed	No	No	No	No
Wait for users to log out	Yes	No	No	No
Wait for ongoing transactions to end	Yes	Yes	No	No
Create a checkpoint and close files	Yes	Yes	Yes	No

Figure 2: Database shutdown actions

Shutdown Timeout

All of the shutdown modes that wait for users to disconnect or for transactions to complete only wait for a limited amount of time. If the events blocking the shutdown have not completed within one hour, the shutdown operation will abort with an ORA-01013 error. You'll get the same error if you attempt to abort a shutdown operation manually by hitting Ctrl-C (Oracle recommends against this). After an ORA-01013 occurs, the instance is in an unpredictable state and you should resubmit the SHUTDOWN command. If subsequent SHUTDOWN commands fail, you must issue a SHUTDOWN ABORT. You can then restart the instance.

Using alert log and trace files

Each server and background process can write to an associated trace file. When an internal error is detected by a process, it dumps information about the error to its trace file. Some of the information written to a trace file is intended for the database administrator, and other information is for Oracle Support Services. Trace file information is also used to tune applications and instances.

All Oracle databases keep an alert log file. The filename is in the form alert_<sid>.log and it will be stored in the $ORACLE_BASE/diag/rdbms/<db_name>/<sid>/trace directory by default. The alert log is a chronological log of messages and errors regarding the database. The file includes the following items:

- All internal errors (ORA-00600), block corruption errors (ORA-01578), and deadlock errors (ORA-00060) that occur
- Administrative operations, such as CREATE, ALTER, and DROP statements and STARTUP, SHUTDOWN, and ARCHIVELOG statements

- Messages and errors relating to the functions of shared server and dispatcher processes
- Errors occurring during the automatic refresh of a materialized view
- The values of all initialization parameters that had nondefault values at the time the database and instance start

The alert log records this information in lieu of displaying the information on the console (although some of these errors might also appear on-screen). Whenever one of the logged operations is successful, a "completed" message and timestamp are written to the alert log. There are two versions of the log maintained: an XML-formatted file and a text-formatted file. Either format of the alert log can be viewed with a text editor. Alternately, you can use the ADRCI command-line utility to view the XML-formatted version of the file.

You should periodically check the alert log and trace files of an instance for errors that require intervention. The alert log and other trace files for background and server processes are written to the Automatic Diagnostic Repository. The ADR location is specified by the DIAGNOSTIC_DEST initialization parameter. Trace file names are operating system specific, but usually include the name of the process writing the file (such as LGWR and RECO).

It's possible to set the maximum size of all trace files except for the alert log. You do so by using the initialization parameter MAX_DUMP_FILE_SIZE. This parameter limits the file to the specified number of operating system blocks when set. The size of an alert log can only be controlled by manually deleting the file (or part of the file) periodically. The database will append to the file indefinitely. Without manual intervention it will only get larger over time. It is safe to delete the alert log while the instance is running. However, it would be advisable to archive a copy of it prior to deletion.

Background processes always write to a trace file when appropriate. For the ARCn background process an initialization parameter can be used to control the amount and type of trace information that is produced. However, the other background processes have no such control capability. Trace files are written for server processes when critical errors occur.

Optionally, you can generate performance statistics for the processing of all SQL statements by setting the initialization parameter SQL_TRACE = TRUE. This causes the SQL trace facility to write these statistics to the Automatic Diagnostic Repository. Individual sessions can enable or disable trace logging by using the SET SQL_TRACE clause of the ALTER SESSION command.

Automatic Diagnostic Repository

In 11G, Oracle introduced the concept of the Automatic Diagnostic Repository (ADR). The ADR is a directory structure for diagnostic files such as traces, dumps, the alert log, health monitor reports, and more. The directory structure supports multiple instances and multiple Oracle products. Each instance of each product will store diagnostic data underneath its own home directory within the ADR. ADR provides a unified directory structure along with consistent diagnostic data formats across products and instances. This plus a unified set of tools enables diagnostic data to be correlated and analyzed across multiple Oracle products.

Because all diagnostic data, including the alert log, is stored in the ADR, the initialization parameters BACKGROUND_DUMP_DEST and USER_DUMP_DEST have been deprecated. They have been replaced by the initialization parameter DIAGNOSTIC_DEST. The DIAGNOSTIC_DEST parameter identifies the directory which serves as the ADR Base location. To determine the locations of trace files, you can query the V$DIAG_INFO view:

```
SELECT name, value
FROM   v$diag_info
WHERE  name LIKE 'Diag%';


NAME              VALUE
-------  ------------------------
Diag Enabled     TRUE
Diag Trace       C:\ORACLEXE\APP\ORACLE\diag\rdbms\xe\xe\trace
Diag Alert       C:\ORACLEXE\APP\ORACLE\diag\rdbms\xe\xe\alert
Diag Incident
C:\ORACLEXE\APP\ORACLE\diag\rdbms\xe\xe\incident
Diag Cdump       C:\oraclexe\app\oracle\diag\rdbms\xe\xe\cdump
```

Some of the locations in the V$DIAG_INFO view include:

- **ADR Base** – Path of ADR base.
- **ADR Home** – Path of ADR home for the current database instance.
- **Diag Trace** – Location of background process trace files, server process trace files, SQL trace files, and the text-formatted version of the alert log.
- **Diag Alert** – Location of the XML-formatted version of the alert log.
- **Default Trace** – File Path to the trace file for the current session.
- **Diag Incident** – File path for incident packages
- **Diag Cdump** – Equivalent to cdump. Location for core dump files.
- **Health Monitor** – Location for health monitor output.

The fault diagnosability infrastructure in Oracle 11G introduces two concepts for the Oracle Database: problems and incidents. A problem is defined as a critical error in the database. Critical errors manifest as internal errors, such as ORA-00600, ORA-07445, or ORA-04031. Problems are tracked in the ADR using a problem key, which is a text string that describes the problem.

An incident is defined as a single occurrence of a problem. When a problem occurs multiple times, an incident is created for each occurrence. Oracle timestamps the incidents and tracks them in the ADR. Incidents are identified by a numeric incident ID, which is unique within the ADR. Each incident in the database generates the following actions:

- An entry is made in the alert log.
- An incident alert is sent to Oracle Enterprise Manager.
- Diagnostic data about the incident is stored in the form of dump files.
- One or more incident dumps are stored in the ADR in a subdirectory created for that incident.

Using data dictionary and dynamic performance views

Dynamic Performance Views

Oracle contains a set of views maintained by the database server called dynamic performance views. The data in these views is continuously updated while a database is in use, and relates primarily to performance. The views act as if they are based on regular database tables, but this is not the case. The views provide data on internal disk structures and memory structures. It's possible to select from these views, but not update or alter them. After installation, only the SYS user or a user with the SYSDBA role can access the dynamic performance views. Only simple queries are supported against the views. Because the information in the V$ views is dynamic, read consistency is not guaranteed when a SELECT is issued against them:

- **V$ Views** – Dynamic performance views are identified by the prefix V_$. However, each has a public synonym using the same name but with the prefix V$. All users should access only the V$ objects, not the V_$ objects. For an instance that is not mounted, only the V$ views that read from memory are accessible. V$ views that read data from disk require that the database be mounted. Some of the V$ views require that the database be open.
- **GV$ Views** – For most V$ views, Oracle has a corresponding GV$ (global V$) view. GV$ views are for use in databases making use of Real Application Clusters. Querying a GV$ view retrieves the V$ view information from all available instances of the database. GV$ views contain an extra column named INST_ID that displays the instance number from which the associated V$ view information was obtained.

Data Dictionary Views

A critical aspect of the Oracle database is its data dictionary. The data dictionary is a read-only set of tables that provides metadata about the database. Among other things, the Oracle data dictionary contains the following:

- Definitions of every schema object in the database, including default values for columns and integrity constraint information

- The amount of space allocated for and currently used by the schema objects
- The names of Oracle Database users, privileges and roles granted to users, and auditing information related to users

The dictionary is central to managing data and objects for every Oracle database. Oracle must access the data dictionary to find information about users, schema objects, and storage structures. The data dictionary is modified every time that a DDL statement is issued in the database.

The data dictionary data is stored inside database tables, just like user data. Because of this, it is possible to query the data using SQL. You can use SELECT statements to locate tables in a schema, determine their structure and any privileges you have on them, see what other objects in the database reference them, and so forth.

The data dictionary consists of two types of objects: base tables and views.

- **Base tables** – The underlying tables of the data dictionary store information about the database. Only Oracle Database should write to and read from these tables through the use of DDL commands. There is very seldom a need for users to access the base tables directly. The information in these tables is normalized and most data is stored in a cryptic format with equally cryptic table names.
- **Views** – Data dictionary views are designed to decode the base table data into useful information using joins and WHERE clauses to simplify the information. Some views are accessible to all database users, and others are intended only for administrators.

The majority of the Oracle data dictionary views are grouped into three sets: DBA, ALL, and USER. By querying the appropriate views, you can access the relevant information. Not all data dictionary view sets will have all three members. For example, the data dictionary contains a DBA_LOCK view but no ALL_LOCK view.

- **DBA_** – These views show data dictionary objects across all schemas. The views are intended to be used by people with Database Administrator-level privileges.

- **ALL_** – These views show data dictionary objects across multiple schemas. The objects shown are filtered based on object level privileges, however. Objects in schemas other than the user querying the view will only be shown if the user has privileges on the object in the other schema. Because the ALL_ views obey the current set of enabled roles, query results will depend on which roles are enabled.
- **USER_** – These views show only data dictionary objects that exist in the schema that is performing the query. The USER views lack the OWNER column that exists in the DBA_ and ALL_ views, since the information is redundant.

The DICTIONARY view contains the names and abbreviated descriptions of all data dictionary views. The following query of this view includes partial sample output:

```
SELECT *
FROM    dictionary
WHERE   table_name LIKE '%ALL_TABLES'
ORDER BY table_name;

TABLE_NAME        COMMENTS
----------------  ------------------------
ALL_ALL_TABLES    Description of all object and relational
                    tables accessible to the user
ALL_TABLES        Description of relational tables accessible
                    to the user
DBA_ALL_TABLES    Description of all object and relational
                    tables in the database
USER_ALL_TABLES   Description of all object and relational
                    tables owned by the users
```

The DUAL Table

The DUAL table in Oracle is a one-column, one row table that is very useful when there is a need to perform an Oracle SQL function that requires a single result that is unrelated to data stored in a user table. The one column in DUAL is called 'DUMMY' and the value in the column for the single row is 'X'. Neither is really important, however, as the table isn't used for what it contains, but for what it does. When making a call to DUAL, the SQL statement contains an operation that needs to be performed. The DUAL table simply acts as a springboard against which to direct the SQL operation so that Oracle can process it and return the results to the user. For example, the following operation returns the current operating system date of the server on which Oracle is installed:

```
SELECT SYSDATE
FROM   dual;

SYSDATE
-----
03-APR-12
```

Configuring the Oracle Network Environment

Oracle Net Services is the element that provides connectivity solutions in distributed computing environments. One component of Oracle Net Services, Oracle Net, enables a network session from a client application to an Oracle Database server. Any time a network session is established between a client application and the database, Oracle Net acts as the data courier. It establishes and maintains the connection between the client application and the database. Throughout the life of the session it is integral in exchanging messages between them. Oracle Net enables connections from traditional client/server applications to Oracle Database servers. Oracle Net resides on both the client and the database server and communicates with TCP/IP to facilitate connectivity and data transfer between the client and the database. The graphic below shows how Oracle Net enables a network connection between a client and a database server. There are several other connection types possible: Java Application connections, Web Client connections through Application Web Server, and others. See the Oracle Database Net Services Administrator's Guide for more details.

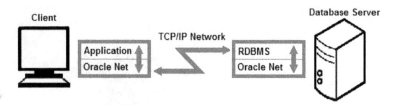

Figure 3: Oracle Net client-server connection

On the client computer, Oracle Net is a background component that facilitates application connections to the database. On the server side, the Oracle Net Listener coordinates connections between the database and client connections. While the most common use of Oracle Net Services is to handle incoming Oracle database connections, it can also be used as an interface to non Oracle data sources (such as SQL Server and DB2) or to access external code libraries via EXTPROC.

Configure and Manage the Oracle Network

The Oracle Database server receives the initial connection through Oracle Net Listener (referred to henceforth as the listener). The listener is an Oracle background process that listens on a specific port for database connection requests. It brokers a client request and hands off the request to the server. The listener is configured with a protocol address. Clients configured to use that protocol address can send connection requests to the listener. Once a connection has been established, the client and Oracle server communicate directly with one another. Stopping the listener will prevent new connections from occurring, but will not affect existing connections.

In order to connect to a database service, clients must use a connect descriptor that provides both the location of the database and the name of the database service. The following example is an Easy Connect descriptor that connects to a database service named ocp.exam.com, and the host ocp-server (by default the port that will be used is 1521): ocp-server/ocp.exam.com

In order for the above connection to work, the database being connected to must have a matching entry in the configuration file tnsnames.ora. The matching entry in that file for the preceding connect descriptor and database service would be:

```
(DESCRIPTION=
(ADDRESS=(PROTOCOL=tcp)(HOST=ocp-server)(PORT=1521))
(CONNECT_DATA=
(SERVICE_NAME=ocp.exam.com)))
```

A connect descriptor is a specially formatted description of the destination for a network connection. It contains the destination service and network route information. The destination service is indicated by name and the network route by the location of the listener through the use of a network address. A connect descriptor is comprised of one or more protocol addresses of the listener and the connect information for the destination service in the tnsnames.ora file. The below example is a connect descriptor for the ocp database.

```
ocp=
(DESCRIPTION=
     (ADDRESS=(PROTOCOL=tcp)
               (HOST=ocp-server)
               (PORT=1521)
     )
     (CONNECT_DATA=(SID=ocp)
                    (SERVICE_NAME=ocp.exam.com)
                    (INSTANCE_NAME=ocp)
     )
)
```

The ADDRESS section contains the following parameters:

- **PROTOCOL** – Identifies the listener protocol address. The protocol 'tcp' is used for TCP/IP.
- **HOST** – Identifies the host name. The host is ocp-server. You can also use an IP address when using the TCP/IP protocol.
- **PORT** – Identifies the port. 1521 is the default port used by Oracle Net.

The CONNECT_DATA section contains the following parameters:

- **SID** – Identifies the SID of the Oracle database. In this case the SID is ocp.
- **SERVICE_NAME** – Identifies the service. The destination service name is a database service named ocp.exam.com. The value for this parameter comes from the SERVICE_NAMES initialization parameter. Generally the SERVICE_NAMES parameter is the global database name.
- **INSTANCE_NAME** – Identifies the database instance. This parameter is optional and defaults to the SID entered during installation or database creation.

When the database is in a dedicated server configuration, the listener starts a separate dedicated server process for each incoming client connection. The server process thus created is dedicated to servicing the one client. When the session is complete, the dedicated server process terminates. The steps for the listener passing a client connection request to a dedicated server process and the establishment of a database session follow:

1. The listener receives a client connection request.
2. The listener starts a dedicated server process, and the dedicated server inherits the connection request from the listener.
3. The client is now connected directly to the dedicated server.
4. The server process checks the client's authentication credentials.
5. If credentials are valid, a session to the database is created.

Oracle Net Configuration Tools

There are three tools available for configuring and managing the Oracle Network.

Oracle Enterprise Manager

OEM allows you to configure Oracle Net Services for any Oracle home across multiple file systems. It also provides common listener administration functions. You can use OEM Net Services Administration page to configure and administer the following:

- Configure listeners to receive client connections.
- Define connect identifiers and map them to connect descriptors to identify the network location of a service.
- Specify the file location of the Oracle Net configuration files.

Oracle Net Manager

Oracle Net Manager enables you to configure Oracle Net Services for an Oracle home on a local client or server host. You can use Oracle Net Manager to configure the following network components:

- Create and configure listeners to receive client connections.
- Define connect identifiers and map them to connect descriptors to identify the network location and identification of a service.
- Configure the ways connect identifiers are resolved to connect descriptors.
- Configure preferences for enabling and configuring Oracle Net features on the client or server.

Oracle Net Configuration Assistant

Oracle Net Configuration Assistant is provided to configure basic network components during installation. It can also be run in standalone mode after installation. The assistant can configure the following:

- Listener names and protocol addresses
- Naming methods the client uses to resolve connect identifiers to connect descriptors
- Net service names in a tnsnames.ora file
- Directory server usage

LSNRCTL

The Listener Control utility is a command-line tool that enables you to administer the listener. The utility is started by the user that owns the Oracle installation (generally the oracle user), or a member of the database administration group. It must be started on the same machine where the listener is running. The basic syntax for this utility is as follows:

```
lsnrctl command [listener_name]
```

For example, the following command starts a listener named lsnr:

```
lsnrctl START lsnr
```

Listener Control utility commands can also be issued from the LSNRCTL> program prompt. To obtain the prompt, enter lsnrctl with no arguments at the operating system command line. This will start the utility, and you can enter commands from the program prompt.

For example:

```
lsnrctl
LSNRCTL> START lsnr
```

Common LSNRCTL commands

- **STOP** – Stop the named listener. Syntax: "LSNRCTL> STOP listener_name".
- **STATUS** – To display basic status information about a listener. Syntax: "LSNRCTL> STATUS listener_name".

- **START** – Start the named listener. Syntax: "LSNRCTL> START listener_name".
- **SHOW** – View the current parameter values for the listener. Syntax: "LSNRCTL> SHOW parameter".
- **SET CURRENT_LISTENER** – Set the name of the listener to administer. Subsequent commands can be issued without supplying the listener name. Syntax: "LSNRCTL> SET CURRENT_LISTENER listener_name".
- **TRACE** – turn on listener tracing.
- **RELOAD** – Re-read listener.ora to use changes without restarting the listener.

A naming method is the means by which a client application resolves a connect identifier to a connect descriptor when attempting to connect to a database service. A connection request is initiated by providing a connect string. The string will consist of a user name and password, along with a connect identifier. The connect identifier can be the connect descriptor or a name that resolves to a connect descriptor. The connect descriptor contains a network route to the service and a database service name or Oracle system identifier (SID). There are four naming methods supported by Oracle:

- **Local Naming** – Stores net service names and their connect descriptors in a localized configuration file named tnsnames.ora, which by default is located in the network/admin subdirectory under the Oracle Database home.
- **Directory Naming** – Stores connect identifiers in a centralized LDAP-compliant directory server to access a database service.
- **Easy Connect Naming** – Enables clients to connect to an Oracle database server by using a TCP/IP connect string consisting of a host name and optional port and service name.
- **External Naming** – Stores net service names in a supported third-party naming service, such as Network Information Service (NIS) External Naming.

There are three key files used to configure Oracle Networking:

- **listener.ora** – Used to configure listeners.
- **tnsnames.ora** – Used when implementing the local naming name resolution method.
- **sqlnet.ora** – Used to select the names resolution method and can set certain parameters.

Using the Oracle Shared Server architecture

Server Processes are required in order for client sessions to communicate with the database. When operating in a dedicated server mode, each client session will map one-to-one with a dedicated server process. Each server process consumes memory and CPU cycles on the Oracle server. For databases with large numbers of users, the CPU and memory load of the server processes can degrade performance of the system.

Making use of shared server architecture will increase the number of clients that can be simultaneously connected to the database by reducing the number of server processes required. No changes to the application are required in order to make use of the shared server architecture. When using a shared server, clients do not communicate directly with a database server process. Client requests are routed to server processes through the use of one or more dispatchers. A single dispatcher can support multiple concurrent connections. Client connections are bound to a virtual circuit, which is a piece of shared memory the dispatcher uses for connection requests and replies. The dispatcher places a virtual circuit into a shared request queue when a request arrives. An idle shared server picks up the virtual circuit from the request queue, services it, places a response in the response queue, and relinquishes the circuit. Once one virtual circuit is released, the shared server will attempt to retrieve another virtual circuit from the request queue. Dispatchers will pick up completed requests from the response queue. Each dispatcher will have its own response queue in the SGA. This architecture allows a small pool of server processes to serve a large number of clients.

The images below show the basic differences between the shared server connection model and the traditional dedicated server connection model.

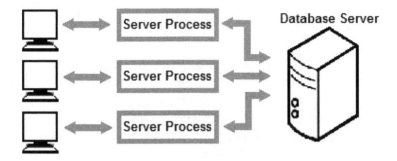

Figure 4: Dedicated Server model

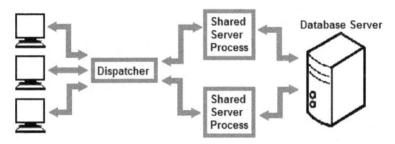

Figure 5: Shared Server model

PGA Differences

The way in which the SGA and PGA memory areas are utilized is different when using shared vs. dedicated connections. When using either dedicated or shared connections, there is a PGA area for each server process. With dedicated connections, the PGA is likewise dedicated to the session and the User Global Area (UGA) for the session is stored within the PGA. The UGA is session memory, which is memory allocated for session variables, such as logon information, and other information required by a database session. The UGA must be available to a database session for the life of the session. When using a shared server connection, the UGA cannot be stored in the PGA, and is therefore stored in the SGA. This enables any shared server process access to it. In the shared server model, the UGA is stored in the large pool or in the shared pool when no large pool exists.

Connection Pooling

In a database application that involves a large number of web clients, many of client sessions may be idle at a given time. The connection pooling feature of Oracle allows the server to timeout an idle session that is using a connection and use the freed connection to service an active session. The idle session remains open, and if it becomes active again, the physical connection is automatically reestablished. This allows larger numbers of concurrent users to be accommodated with existing hardware.

Bypassing Shared Connections

There are situations where users and administrators should explicitly connect to an instance using a dedicated server process:

- When running batch processing where there is little or no idle time for the server process.
- When using Recovery Manager (RMAN) to back up, restore, or recover a database.
- When starting or shutting down the database.
- When performing most database management activities.

If the Oracle Database is configured for shared server, in order to obtain a dedicated server connection, users must connect using a net service name that has been configured to use a dedicated server. The net service name value for the dedicated connection should include the SERVER=DEDICATED clause in the connect descriptor.

Managing Database Storage Structures

The primary reason that a database exists is to store data. Understanding the various aspects of Oracle data storage is essential to being an effective database administrator. This section will detail the information you need to know for the test regarding the physical and logical storage structures used by the database.

Physical storage structures are the files that store the data.

- Data files
- Control files
- Online redo log files

Logical storage structures are what give the database fine-grained control of disk space use:

- Data blocks
- Extents
- Segments
- Tablespaces

Overview of tablespaces and datafiles

Logical storage structures were briefly defined earlier. The following list reviews the logical structures Oracle uses, from smallest to largest and adds some additional rules.

- **Data blocks** – At the finest level of granularity, data is stored in data blocks. One data block corresponds to a specific number of bytes on disk.
- **Extents** – An extent is a specific number of logically contiguous data blocks, obtained in a single allocation, and used to store a specific type of information. A single extent cannot span more than one data file.
- **Segments** – A segment is a set of extents allocated for a user object (for example, a table or index), undo data, or temporary data. A segment can span multiple data files, but exists in only a

single tablespace. Any given database object is made up of a single segment.

- **Tablespaces** – A database is divided into logical storage units called tablespaces. A tablespace is the logical container for a segment. Each tablespace contains at least one data file. A tablespace can belong to only a single database. A data file can belong to only a single tablespace.

Table data is made up of rows. Rows are stored in a table segment, in an extent, and ultimately in a data block. When viewed from the block level, what is stored is specifically called a row piece. It has this name because it is possible for a row to be larger than a single block, in which case the row will be split into two or more pieces in multiple data blocks. In some situations, a row may end up stored in multiple blocks even if the sum of all the pieces is less than the block size. Oracle data blocks have an internal structure that allows the database to keep track of the data and free space in the block. The formats for table, index, or table cluster data blocks are all very similar. The contents of a data block are:

- **Block header** – The header contains general information, including disk address and segment type.
- **Table directory** – Contains metadata about tables whose rows are stored in this block for heap-organized tables. It is possible for multiple tables to store rows in the same block.
- **Row directory** – Describes the location of rows in the data portion of the block for a heap-organized table.
- **Row Format** – This part of the block is what contains the actual table rows or index key entries. Every row has a row format that enables the database to track the data in the row. Rows are stored as variable-length records.
- **Row Header** – The row header is used to manage the row piece stored in the block. It contains information such as the columns in the row piece, pointers to pieces of the row located in other data blocks, and cluster keys.

Oracle uses rowids to uniquely identify every row in the database. A rowid holds the information that the database needs to access a row. Rowids are not physically stored in the database table. They are calculated from the file and block on which the data is stored.

Create and manage tablespaces

The steps for creating tablespaces vary slightly depending on the operating system. For any operating system, however, you must create a directory structure to store the datafiles for your tablespace as the first step. For most operating systems, you will specify the size and complete filenames for the datafiles that will make up the tablespace either when you are creating a new tablespace or adding files to an existing tablespace. In either case, the database automatically allocates and formats the datafiles.

There are three variants of the CREATE TABLESPACE command. To perform any of the three, you must have been granted the CREATE TABLESPACE system privilege.

- **CREATE TABLESPACE** – Creates a tablespace to be used to store permanent database objects such as tables and indexes.
- **CREATE TEMPORARY TABLESPACE** – Creates a tablespace that is used for temporary segments such as sort segments or segments assigned to temporary tables.
- **CREATE UNDO TABLESPACE** – Used to create an undo tablespace. An undo tablespace will contain nothing but undo records. These records are used to roll back changes to the database for recovery, read consistency, or when requested by a ROLLBACK statement.

Once a tablespace has been created, you can use the ALTER TABLESPACE or ALTER DATABASE statements to alter it (if you have the ALTER TABLESPACE or ALTER DATABASE system privileges).

Space management in tablespaces

Locally Managed Tablespaces

A tablespace that is locally managed uses bitmaps within the tablespace itself to track all extent information. Local management has several benefits over traditional tablespaces where this information is stored in the data dictionary:

- Space allocations and deallocations modify locally managed resources. This makes them fast and concurrent, resulting in enhanced performance.
- Locally managed temporary tablespaces do not generate any undo or redo.
- If the AUTOALLOCATE clause is specified, the database automatically selects the appropriate extent size.
- Reliance on the data dictionary is reduced, reducing contention in times of high activity to tables.
- There is no need to coalesce free extents.

Any tablespace can be locally managed, including SYSTEM and SYSAUX. There are maintenance procedures in the DBMS_SPACE_ADMIN package specific to locally managed tablespaces.

The syntax to create a locally managed tablespace, is the keyword LOCAL in the EXTENT MANAGEMENT clause of the CREATE TABLESPACE statement. The default value for new permanent tablespaces is 'EXTENT MANAGEMENT LOCAL AUTOALLOCATE'. Specifying this clause is optional unless you do not want local management or you want to use the UNIFORM keyword rather than AUTOALLOCATE. When the AUTOALLOCATE keyword is used, the database will manage extents automatically. If you want the tablespace to utilize uniform extents of a specific size, you must specify the UNIFORM keyword. The two commands below will have identical effects:

```
CREATE TABLESPACE ocpts DATAFILE
'/u02/oracle/data/ocpts01.dbf' SIZE 50M
EXTENT MANAGEMENT LOCAL AUTOALLOCATE;

CREATE TABLESPACE ocpts DATAFILE
'/u02/oracle/data/ocpts01.dbf' SIZE 50M;
```

There are two methods that Oracle Database can use to manage segment space in a locally managed tablespace. Manual space management uses freelists to manage free space in a segment. Automatic segment space management uses bitmaps. Automatic segment space management is more efficient method, and is the default for all new permanent, locally managed tablespaces. You can explicitly enable it with the SEGMENT SPACE MANAGEMENT AUTO clause:

```
CREATE TABLESPACE ocpts DATAFILE
'/u02/oracle/data/ocpts01.dbf' SIZE 50M
EXTENT MANAGEMENT LOCAL AUTOALLOCATE
SEGMENT SPACE MANAGEMENT AUTO;
```

Dictionary Managed Tablespaces

Dictionary-managed tablespaces that existed prior to locally managed tablespaces are still available. However, they exist for backward compatibility. You're very unlikely to see anything about them on the test. Even finding documentation on them is difficult because Oracle **really** wants you to use locally managed tablespaces. I mention them here only to note that there is a reason for not having a section describing their behavior. One point that might come up is that there is a procedure in the DBMS_SPACE_ADMIN package called TABLESPACE_MIGRATE_TO_LOCAL that will allow you to convert dictionary-managed tablespaces to locally managed tablespaces. For more information on using this procedure, consult the Oracle Database Administrator's Guide.

Compression

When you create a tablespace, it's possible to specify that all tables created in it be compressed by default. When adding the clause, you must specify the type of table compression. This is done with the DEFAULT keyword, followed by the compression type to be used. There are four different compression options (although the difference between the QUERY and ARCHIVE compression types is fuzzy):

- **DEFAULT COMPRESS [BASIC]** – Basic table compression compresses data inserted by direct path load only and supports limited data types and SQL operations.
- **DEFAULT COMPRESS FOR OLTP** – All tables created in the tablespace will use OLTP compression, unless otherwise specified. OLTP table compression is intended for OLTP applications and compresses data manipulated by any SQL operation.
- **DEFAULT COMPRESS FOR QUERY [LOW|HIGH]** – This compression method can result in high CPU overhead and works best for direct-path load. Rows inserted without using direct-path insert and updated rows go to a block with a less compressed format and have lower compression level.

- **DEFAULT COMPRESS FOR ARCHIVE [LOW|HIGH]** – This compression method can result in high CPU overhead and works best for direct-path load. Rows inserted without using direct-path insert and updated rows go to a block with a less compressed format and have lower compression level.

You can get more information on the compression types from the Oracle Database Administrator's Guide. Tables created in a tablespace with the compression option enabled will default to that method. However, you can create tables uncompressed or using a different method by supplying a compression clause in the CREATE TABLE statement. If you alter the default compression in a tablespace, all new tables created will default to the new method, but existing tables are unchanged.

Altering Tablespaces

The ALTER TABLESPACE command can be used to change many aspects of existing tablespaces:

- Data file operations, including adding new ones. Existing datafiles can be increased in size, have their AUTOEXTEND setting changed, or renamed. For temporary tablespaces, it's also possible to take files offline.
- Altering tablespace availability (ONLINE/OFFLINE).
- Making a tablespace read-only or read/write.
- Change the name of a tablespace.
- Shrinking files in temporary tablespaces.

Dropping Tablespaces

You can drop a tablespace and its contents from the database using the DROP TABLESPACE command. You must have the DROP TABLESPACE system privilege in order to do this. When a tablespace is dropped, the file pointers in the control file of the associated database are removed. It is possible to delete the operating system files associated with the dropped tablespace simultaneously. If you do not delete the datafiles using the DROP TABLESPACE command, you must later delete the files using operating system commands. A tablespace cannot be dropped if it contains any active segments. It is recommended that you take the tablespace offline before dropping it.

Oracle Managed Files

The Oracle Managed Files feature is a method for automating the administration of data files in an Oracle Database. It removes the need for the DBA to directly manage the operating system files that make up an Oracle Database. When making use of Oracle Managed Files, the DBA will specify one or more directories on the file system. The database will make use of those directories at the same time that it creates, names, and manages files at the database object level. In practice, this means that when creating a tablespace, you will specify on the logical aspects of the tablespace, the DATAFILE clause of the CREATE TABLESPACE command will not be used. Making use of Oracle Managed Files removes some control over how files are laid out on the disks. This, in turn, means that you lose some I/O tuning ability. To use OMF, you must set the following parameters:

- **DB_CREATE_FILE_DEST** – Sets the default location for all data files.
- **DB_CREATE_ONLINE_LOG_DEST_n** – Sets the default location for online redo log files.
- **DB_RECOVERY_FILE_DEST** – Sets the default location for archived redo and backup files.

Oracle Automatic Storage Management

Oracle Automatic Storage Management (ASM) is storage solution for Oracle Database files. It acts as a volume manager to provide a file system for the exclusive use of the database. When using ASM, partitioned disks are assigned to ASM with specifications for striping and mirroring. The ASM instance will then manage the disk space and distribute the load to optimize performance. ASM provides several benefits over using standard datafiles:

- Simplifies operations such as creating databases and managing disk space
- Distributes data across physical disks to provide uniform performance
- Rebalances data automatically after storage configuration changes

The logical storage elements of an Oracle ASM instance are:

- **ASM Disks** – A storage device that is provisioned to an Oracle ASM disk group. It can be a physical disk or partition, a Logical Unit Number (LUN) from a storage array, a logical volume, or a network-attached file.
- **ASM Disk Groups** – A collection of Oracle ASM disks managed as a logical unit.
- **ASM Files** – A file stored in an Oracle ASM disk group. The database can store data files, control files, online redo log files, and other types of files as Oracle ASM files.
- **ASM Extents** – The raw storage used to hold the contents of an Oracle ASM file. An ASM file consists of one or more file extents and an ASM extent consists of one or more ASM allocation units.
- **ASM Allocation Units** – The fundamental unit of allocation within a disk group.
- **ASM Instances** – A special Oracle instance that manages Oracle ASM disks. They manage the metadata of the disk group and provide file layout information to the database instances.

Dictionary Views

There are several dictionary views, both static and dynamic, with information on tablespaces, their contents, and associated data files.

- **DBA_TABLESPACES** – Descriptions of all tablespaces.
- **DBA_SEGMENTS** – Information about segments within all tablespaces.
- **DBA_EXTENTS** – Information about data extents within all tablespaces.
- **DBA_FREE_SPACE** – Information about free extents within all tablespaces.

- **DBA_TEMP_FREE_SPACE** – Displays the total allocated and free space in each temporary tablespace.
- **DBA_DATA_FILES** – Shows files (datafiles) belonging to tablespaces.
- **DBA_TEMP_FILES** – Shows files (tempfiles) belonging to temporary tablespaces.
- **DBA_TS_QUOTAS** – Lists tablespace quotas for all users.

- **V$TABLESPACE** – Name and number of all tablespaces from the control file.
- **V$ENCRYPTED_TABLESPACES** – Name and encryption algorithm of all encrypted tablespaces.
- **V$DATAFILE** – Information about all datafiles, including tablespace number of owning tablespace.
- **V$TEMPFILE** – Information about all tempfiles, including tablespace number of owning tablespace.
- **V$SORT_SEGMENT** – Information about every sort segment in a given instance.
- **V$TEMPSEG_USAGE** – Describes temporary (sort) segment usage by user for temporary or permanent tablespaces.

Administering User Security

An Oracle database is designed to have dozens, hundreds, possibly thousands of users accessing it. Unless the database is being used purely for testing purposes, the data within it is almost certain to be important and at least some portions of the data will likely be confidential. For these reasons and more, it is important to have a security policy for every database. That policy will establish means to protect the data it contains. This protection involves both keeping sensitive data from being accessed inappropriately and keeping data from being altered or destroyed either accidentally or intentionally.

Create and manage database user accounts

The data in an Oracle database cannot be accessed without a connection to the database. In order to make a connection to the database, it is necessary to supply a valid database user name. Oracle user names are established by database administrators, and information about the user is stored in the data dictionary. The CREATE USER statement allows you to add new user accounts to an Oracle database. In order to create a user, you must have the CREATE USER system privilege. This is a powerful privilege, and is normally restricted to a database administrator or security administrator. The various elements that should be defined when creating a user are:

- **USERNAME** – User names in a database must be unique. They also share a namespace with roles, which means that you cannot have an identical username and role in a single database. When a user is created in a database, an associated schema is created of the same name.
- **AUTHENTICATION** – In order to connect to the database, each user must be authenticated. Most commonly, the connecting user must supply the correct password to the database in order to connect. The IDENTIFIED BY clause in the CREATE USER statement is used to specify a password.
- **DEFAULT TABLESPACE** – Each user should have a default tablespace. When a user creates a schema object and the DDL

statement does not specify a tablespace, the user's default tablespace is where it will be created. If not specified, the default tablespaces for a user will be the SYSTEM tablespace. SYSTEM is a terrible place for users to create objects. For any user that will be creating objects, you should assign a default tablespace other than SYSTEM. It is also possible to change the default tablespace used by Oracle from SYSTEM to another tablespace. After changing the database default tablespace, all non-SYSTEM users who had been assigned the old default tablespace will automatically be assigned to the new default tablespace. All objects subsequently created by those users will be stored in the tablespace by default.

- **QUOTA** – By default, users have no quota on any tablespace in the database. A quota grants users a set amount of space for objects in a given tablespace. For users that will be creating objects in the database, you should assign a quota to them. During user creation, you can assign a quota to a single tablespace (presumably their default tablespace) or to more than one tablespaces by repeating the quota line.
- **TEMPORARY TABLESPACE** – Users need to make use of a temporary tablespace when performing operations that create temporary segments. Temporary segments are created by the system when performing sort or join operations. After changing the database default temporary tablespace, all non-SYSTEM users who had been assigned the old default temporary tablespace will automatically be assigned to the new default temporary tablespace.
- **PROFILE** – A profile is a set of limits on database resources and password access to the database. If you do not specify a profile, then Oracle Database assigns the user a default profile.

The following CREATE USER statement combines all of the elements described above to create a user with a password, default and temporary tablespaces, quota on two tablespaces, and a profile:

```
CREATE USER ocpuser
IDENTIFIED BY dumbpassword
DEFAULT TABLESPACE user_ts
QUOTA 10M ON test_ts
QUOTA 50M ON user_ts
TEMPORARY TABLESPACE temp_ts
```

```
PROFILE geek;
```

A newly created user cannot connect to the database until the account has been granted the CREATE SESSION system privilege. As a general rule, immediately after creating a user account, an administrator will grant that to the user.

```
GRANT CREATE SESSION TO ocpuser;
```

Altering User Accounts

All of the above items, with the exception of the username, can be changed after the user account exists with the ALTER USER command. All of the options that can be changed by the ALTER USER command except one require the ALTER USER privilege. The exception is that any user can change their own password. The syntax for this is:

```
ALTER USER ocpuser IDENTIFIED BY alsodumbpassword;
```

As with the CREATE USER privilege, only database administrators or security administrators should have this system privilege. Allowing modifications to user accounts is an incredibly powerful and dangerous ability. Users with this privilege can change any user's password, or set tablespace quotas for a user on any tablespace in the database. You can use the ALTER USER statement to change individual values of a user, or multiple values at once, as in the following example:

```
ALTER USER ocpuser
IDENTIFIED EXTERNALLY
DEFAULT TABLESPACE data_ts
TEMPORARY TABLESPACE temp_ts
QUOTA 5M ON data_ts
PROFILE peon;
```

Predefined Administrative Accounts

There are two administrative accounts that are automatically created for every Oracle database:

- **SYS** – The user SYS is automatically created and granted the DBA role. All of the base tables and views for the database data dictionary are stored in the schema SYS. SYS is in effect the owner of the entire data dictionary. All of the tables and views in the data dictionary are critical to the function of Oracle Database. They should never be modified directly by anyone, and no tables should ever be created in the SYS schema. The SYS account should never be accessed by database users and administrators should avoid using it more than is absolutely necessary.
- **SYSTEM** – The user SYSTEM is also automatically created and granted the DBA role. The SYSTEM account is only slightly less critical to the functioning of the database than SYS. It is used to

create tables and views that display administrative information, and internal tables and views used by various Oracle Database options and tools. As with SYS, the SYSTEM schema ideally should not be used to store non-standard objects of your own.

User Passwords in 11G

New with Oracle 11G, user account passwords are case sensitive by default. You can alter this behavior using the SEC_CASE_SENSITIVE_LOGON initialization parameter. Only users with the ALTER SYSTEM privilege can alter the value of this parameter. Set it to TRUE to enable case sensitivity or FALSE to disable case sensitivity. Oracle strongly recommends that you leave case sensitivity in passwords enabled.

Oracle supplies a basic password complexity verification function with 11G called VERIFY_FUNCTION_11G. The VERIFY_FUNCTION_11G function is created by running the UTLPWDMG.SQL script. You can customize this function to meet your own requirements. Oracle recommends that you do so, in fact. By default, password complexity verification is not enabled. To enable password complexity verification you must perform the following steps:

- Log in to SQL*Plus with administrative privileges and run the UTLPWDMG.SQL script (or your variant thereof) to create the password complexity function in the SYS schema.
- In the default profile or the user profile, set the PASSWORD_VERIFY_FUNCTION setting to either the sample password complexity function in the UTLPWDMG.SQL script, or to your customized function. Use one of the following methods:
  - ✓ Log in to SQL*Plus with administrator privileges and use the CREATE PROFILE or ALTER PROFILE statement to enable the function.
    ```
    ALTER PROFILE default LIMIT
      PASSWORD_VERIFY_FUNCTION verify_function_11G;
    ```

✓ In Oracle Enterprise Manager, go to the Edit Profiles page and then under Complexity, select the name of the password complexity function from the Complexity function list.

Oracle 11G can make use of a cryptographic hashing algorithm based on SHA-1. This helps protect against password-based security threats by including support for mixed case characters, special characters, and multibyte characters in passwords. The SHA-1 hashing algorithm also adds salt to each password when it is hashed, which provides additional protection.

Grant and revoke privileges

There are two broad classes of privileges that can be granted to a user or role:

- **System Privileges** – Provide the ability to perform a task that has a scope beyond that of a single database object. Many of the system privileges have a scope of the entire database, for example ALTER USER or CREATE ROLLBACK SEGMENT. Others have a scope that is just for the schema of the user who has been granted the privilege, for example CREATE TABLE or CREATE PROCEDURE.
- **Object Privileges** – Provide the ability to perform a task on a specific database object. For example, GRANT SELECT ON employees.

Some examples of System Privileges are:

- **CREATE TABLE** – Create a table in the grantee's schema.
- **CREATE ANY TABLE** – Create a table in any schema.
- **ALTER ANY TABLE** – Alter any table or view in any schema.
- **DELETE ANY TABLE** – Delete rows from tables in any schema.
- **DROP ANY TABLE** – Drop (or truncate) tables in any schema.
- **INSERT ANY TABLE** – Insert rows into tables in any schema.
- **CREATE ANY INDEX** – Create an index on any table in any schema.
- **ALTER ANY INDEX** – Alter indexes in any schema.

Some examples of Object Privileges are:

- **ALTER** – Right to use ALTER TABLE to change a given table.
- **INDEX** – Right to use the CREATE INDEX command on a given table.
- **INSERT** – Right to INSERT new rows into a given table.
- **SELECT** – Right to SELECT data from a given table.
- **UPDATE** – Right to UPDATE data in a given table.
- **DELETE** – Right to DELETE rows from a given table.

Administrator-Level System Privileges

There are several system privileges that provide an account with very high-level capabilities. These privileges should be granted rarely, and only to trusted users:

- **SYSDBA** – Allows a user to effectively connect as the SYS user. The account has full control over the database.
- **SYSOPER** – Allows a user to start up, shut down, and administer a database instance.
- **SYSASM** – Allows a user to start up, shut down, and administer an ASM instance.
- **RESTRICTED SESSION** – User can login when database is opened in restricted session mode.
- **ALTER DATABASE** – Allows a user to issue ALTER DATABASE commands.
- **ALTER SYSTEM** – Allows a user to issue ALTER SYSTEM commands.
- **GRANT ANY PRIVILEGE** – Allows a user to grant any system privilege to other accounts.
- **GRANT ANY OBJECT PRIVILEGE** – Allows a user to grant any privilege on objects in the database regardless of schema.

ANY keyword

A significant percentage of system privileges have two similar commands, with and without the ANY keyword (i.e. CREATE TABLE vs. CREATE ANY TABLE). The ANY keyword means that the grant is not schema-specific. When a user is granted CREATE TABLE, they are able to create tables in their own schema. However, when granted CREATE ANY TABLE, they can

Oracle Certification Prep

create tables in any user's schema. The ANY keyword makes the privilege much less restrictive and therefore much more dangerous.

WITH ADMIN OPTION

System privileges may optionally be made using the WITH ADMIN option (i.e. GRANT ALTER ANY TABLE WITH ADMIN OPTION). This option allows the user granted this privilege to grant it to other users in turn. In fact, they can grant the privilege to a third user 'WITH ADMIN OPTION' who could in turn grant it to a fourth and so on. If the system privilege is later revoked from a user who was given the admin option, any grants they made of this system privilege are not revoked. The revoke of system privileges does not cascade.

WITH GRANT OPTION

Object privileges have a similar clause called the WITH GRANT OPTION. When an object privilege is granted to a user with this option, that user can grant the object privilege to other users. One distinct difference between the two is that if the privilege is revoked from a user given the WITH GRANT OPTION, any privileges that the user granted are also revoked. The revoke of object privileges does cascade.

Grant privileges on tables

In order to access tables that are owned by another schema, you must have been granted access to do so. This might be through a system privilege such as SELECT ANY TABLE, or by a grant on the table itself by the schema owner, or another database user that has privileges that allow it to grant the required access. Until a privilege has been granted, Oracle will treat attempts to SELECT from it as if the table does not even exist.

```
SELECT *
FROM   hr.regions;

ORA-00942: table or view does not exist
00942. 00000 -  "table or view does not exist"
*Cause:
*Action:
```

If the SELECT privilege is granted to the querying schema, then the above statement will succeed:

```
GRANT SELECT ON hr.regions TO ocpguru;

GRANT succeeded.

SELECT *
FROM    hr.regions;

REGION_ID REGION_NAME
--------- ---------------
        1 Europe
        2 Americas
        3 Asia
        4 Middle East and Africa
```

To remove a privilege that has been granted, the REVOKE statement is required:

```
REVOKE SELECT ON hr.regions FROM ocpguru;

REVOKE succeeded.
```

QUOTAS

Users who will be creating objects need to be assigned a quota on the tablespace(s) where those objects will be created. On account creation, users will have zero quota on all tablespaces by default. Quota allows users to consume a limited amount of space in a designated location. There is no need to grant users quota on temporary tablespaces or on undo tablespaces.

If at some point you alter a user's quota to be less than their previous one, then the following rules apply:

- If the new tablespace quota has already been exceeded, existing objects cannot be allocated more space until their combined space is less than the new quota.
- If the new quota has not been exceeded, then the user's objects can be allocated space up to the new quota.

The alternative to granting a quota to a user is granting the UNLIMITED TABLESPACE privilege or the RESOURCE role (which contains that privilege). However, in that case, you have lost control over how much space the user account can consume and which tablespace it will be used in. Quota is a much more controlled means of giving users access to space. The UNLIMITED TABLESPACE privilege overrides all explicit tablespace quotas for the user. If you later revoke the privilege, then you must explicitly grant quotas to individual tablespaces. You can grant this privilege only to users, not to roles.

Create and manage roles

A role is a container for a set of privileges. It is not in and of itself a privilege. When created, a new role contains no privileges and granting it to a user would confer no additional rights within the database. Once privileges have been added to a role and the role granted to a user, the user can then enable it and exercise the privileges granted to it. A default role is automatically enabled for a user when the user creates a session. You can assign a user zero or more default roles. Privileges granted to a schema are part of that schema even when the user is not logged in to the database. By contrast, the privileges a schema has from a role are only in effect while the user has an open database session and the role is enabled. Non-default roles must be enabled manually by issuing the SET ROLE command. Non-default roles can be password protected by adding the IDENTIFIED BY clause when creating the role.

Both system and object privileges can be granted to roles, and those roles subsequently granted to users. Roles are useful for quickly and easily granting multiple permissions to users. There are also a number of roles that have been pre-defined by Oracle. You can grant these roles to users if you wish. However, Oracle recommends creating your own roles that contain only the privileges pertaining to your requirements so that you have more control. Oracle has been known to change the privileges in pre-defined roles. They did so with the CONNECT role, which originally had nine privileges, but now only has the CREATE SESSION privilege.

```
CREATE ROLE hr_authority;
role HR_AUTHORITY created.

GRANT SELECT ON employees TO hr_authority;
GRANT succeeded.
```

```
GRANT UPDATE ON employees TO hr_authority;
GRANT succeeded.

GRANT DELETE ON employees TO hr_authority;
GRANT succeeded.

GRANT hr_authority to jjones;
GRANT succeeded.
```

Predefined Roles

- **CONNECT** – Has the CONNECT SESSION privilege.
- **RESOURCE** – Has privileges that allows users to create tables, indexes, triggers, sequences and more in their own schema. It also provides UNLIMITED TABLESPACE to the user.
- **DBA** – This role contains the vast majority of database system privileges. The DBA role should be granted only to actual database administrators.
- **SELECT_CATALOG_ROLE** – Allows a user to view the data dictionary but does not allow viewing of data.
- **SCHEDULER_ADMIN** – Provides the system privileges required to manage the Oracle Scheduler.
- **PUBLIC** – Every user has this role. It is a placeholder where you can grant privileges that should be available to every user in the database. After granting a privilege to PUBLIC, the privilege is freely available to every single database user <u>without exception</u>. This must always be used with caution, especially when dealing with system privileges.

Create and manage profiles

A profile is a named set of resource limits and password parameters that restrict database usage and instance resources for a user. A user account can have no profile assigned or one profile – no more. It is also possible to assign a default profile to all accounts, and specific profiles to individuals (i.e. any user that doesn't have a specific profile assigned will use the default). Profiles are not required and should be used when there is a need to limit resources in your database. Generally several profiles will be created for different classes of users to match their resource needs and the appropriate profile will then be assigned to each user.

The resource limits defined by profiles are only enforced when resource limitation is enabled for the associated database. It is common for administrators to define and assign elaborate profiles for their users but not enable RESOURCE_LIMIT, and then wonder why nothing changes. You can enable resource limitation by using the ALTER SYSTEM command. Password parameters exist in profiles, but do not require resource limitation to be in effect to be enabled.

Profiles can be assigned to users only – not to roles or other profiles. Any profile assignment will only affect future sessions of a given user. The DBA_PROFILES view contains information about profiles in the database. To create, assign, and drop profiles, you need the CREATE PROFILE, ALTER USER, and DROP PROFILE privileges respectively. If a profile has been assigned to users, you must use the CASCADE option to drop the profile. If a profile with assigned users is dropped, any sessions currently connected will continue to have the resource limits imposed until their next connection to the database.

Some of the resources that can be controlled via profiles are:

Kernel Resources
- **CONNECT_TIME** – Allowable connect time per session in minutes
- **CPU_PER_CALL** – Maximum CPU time per call (100ths of a second)
- **CPU_PER_SESSION** – Maximum CPU time per session (100ths of a second)
- **IDLE_TIME** – Allowed idle time before user is disconnected (minutes)
- **LOGICAL_READS_PER_CALL** – Maximum number of database blocks read per call
- **LOGICAL_READS_PER_SESSION** – Maximum number of database blocks read per session
- **PRIVATE_SGA** – Maximum integer bytes of private space in the SGA
- **SESSIONS_PER_USER** – Number of concurrent multiple sessions allowed per user

Password Resources

- **FAILED_LOGIN_ATTEMPTS** – The number of failed attempts to log in to the user account before the account is locked.
- **PASSWORD_GRACE_TIME** – The number of days after the grace period begins during which a warning is issued and login is allowed. If the password is not changed during the grace period, the password expires.
- **PASSWORD_LIFE_TIME** – The number of days the same password can be used for authentication.
- **PASSWORD_LOCK_TIME** – the number of days an account will be locked after the specified number of consecutive failed.
- **PASSWORD_REUSE_MAX** – The number of times a password must be changed before it can be reused.
- **PASSWORD_REUSE_TIME** – The number of days between reuses of a password.

The example below shows the creation of a basic profile limiting the user to a single connection to the database, an idle time of 30 minutes, and a total connect time to 600 minutes (10 hours):

```
CREATE PROFILE ocptest LIMIT
SESSIONS_PER_USER 1
IDLE_TIME 30
CONNECT_TIME 600;
```

There are several data dictionary views that provide information on profiles:

- **DBA_PROFILES** – Displays all profiles and their limits
- **USER_PASSWORD_LIMITS** – Describes the password profile parameters that are assigned to the user
- **USER_RESOURCE_LIMITS** – Displays the resource limits for the current user

The DBA_PROFILE view lists all profiles in the database and associated settings for each limit in each profile. The example below displays information on the OCPTEST profile:

```
SELECT resource_name, resource_type, limit
FROM   dba_profiles
WHERE  profile = 'OCPTEST';

RESOURCE_NAME                RESOURCE_TYPE LIMIT
-------------------------    ------------- -------
COMPOSITE_LIMIT             KERNEL        DEFAULT
FAILED_LOGIN_ATTEMPTS       PASSWORD      DEFAULT
PASSWORD_LIFE_TIME          PASSWORD      DEFAULT
PASSWORD_REUSE_TIME         PASSWORD      DEFAULT
PASSWORD_REUSE_MAX          PASSWORD      DEFAULT
PASSWORD_VERIFY_FUNCTION    PASSWORD      DEFAULT
PASSWORD_LOCK_TIME          PASSWORD      DEFAULT
PASSWORD_GRACE_TIME         PASSWORD      DEFAULT
PRIVATE_SGA                 KERNEL        DEFAULT
CONNECT_TIME                KERNEL        600
IDLE_TIME                   KERNEL        30
LOGICAL_READS_PER_CALL      KERNEL        DEFAULT
LOGICAL_READS_PER_SESSION   KERNEL        DEFAULT
CPU_PER_CALL                KERNEL        DEFAULT
CPU_PER_SESSION             KERNEL        DEFAULT
SESSIONS_PER_USER           KERNEL        1
```

Managing Data and Concurrency

Any multiuser DBMS must be able to handle concurrency. Concurrency is the simultaneous access of the same data by multiple users. In a database without concurrency controls, users could make changes to data that would compromise data integrity. For example, if two users were to simultaneously update the same row, the end results would be indeterminate. One way of handling concurrency in a multi-user environment when users try to access the same data, is to make users wait. From a performance and usability standpoint, however, the ideal is to make wait time either nonexistent or negligible. The goal is for SQL statements that modify data to proceed with minimal interference. Oracle uses locks to control concurrent access to data. A lock is a mechanism that prevents one transaction from acting destructively on a second transaction accessing a shared resource. Locks help ensure data integrity while allowing maximum concurrent access to data.

A closely related concept to concurrency is data consistency. Data consistency means that each user in the database must see a consistent view of the data. This includes uncommitted changes made by a user's own transactions and committed transactions of other users. The database must prevent what are called 'dirty reads'. This occurs when one transaction sees uncommitted changes made by another concurrent transaction. Oracle enforces statement-level read consistency. This guarantees that data returned by a query is committed and consistent with respect to a single point in time. This point may be the time at which the statement was opened or the time the transaction began. It's also possible for Oracle to provide read consistency to all queries in a transaction. This is transaction-level read consistency and ensures each statement in a transaction sees data from the time at which the transaction began.

All Oracle transactions comply with the basic properties of a database transaction, known as ACID properties. ACID is an acronym for the following:

- **Atomicity** – All tasks of a transaction are performed or none of them are. There are no partial transactions.
- **Consistency** – The transaction takes the database from one consistent state to another consistent state.

- **Isolation** – The effect of a transaction is not visible to other transactions until the transaction is committed.
- **Durability** – Changes made by committed transactions are permanent. After a transaction completes, the database ensures through its recovery mechanisms that changes from the transaction are not lost.

Monitor and resolve locking conflicts

Locks are mechanisms that prevent destructive interaction between transactions accessing the same resource. Some of the resources that Oracle locks are user objects, such as tables and rows. There are also locks against system objects such as shared data structures in memory and data dictionary rows. There are three broad classes of locks (listed below). For the purposes of this exam, we'll deal only with DML locks.

- **DML Locks** – Protect data. For example, table locks lock entire tables, while row locks lock selected rows.
- **DDL Locks** – Protect the structure of schema objects—for example, the dictionary definitions of tables and views.
- **System Locks** – Protect internal database structures such as data files. Latches, mutexes, and internal locks are entirely automatic

As a general rule, there is no user-interaction in obtaining locks. When executing SQL, Oracle automatically determines what locks are required and obtains them. However, there is also a capability to manually obtain locks on user objects. A transaction might lock a single row, multiple rows, or an entire table. Oracle will always choose the lowest-level of locking possible. Also, locks in Oracle do not escalate. Some databases will 'escalate' row level locking to a table lock once a certain number or percentage of rows in a table are locked. This does not happen in Oracle. Once one session obtains a lock on a particular resource, no other session may modify that resource until the transaction holding the lock has completed. However, the resource is still available for read operations. Query operations never obtain a lock and are not blocked by them.

A DML lock, or data lock, guarantees the integrity of table data accessed concurrently by multiple users. DML locks prevent destructive interference of simultaneous conflicting DML or DDL operations. When issuing a DML statement, Oracle will automatically acquire a row lock and a table lock:

Row Locks (TX)

A row lock, also called a TX lock, is obtained for a single row of table. A transaction will require a row lock for every row being modified. The row lock exists until the transaction commits or rolls back. These locks act to queue transactions so that no two transactions modify the same row at the same time. Oracle will always lock a modified row in exclusive mode. Other transactions cannot modify the row until the first transaction ends. Row locking provides the best possible concurrency. Oracle stores lock information in the data block that contains the locked row.

Table Locks (TM)

A table lock, also called a TM lock, is acquired by a transaction when a table is modified by a DML statement. DML operations require table locks to reserve DML access to the table on behalf of a transaction and to prevent conflicting DDL operations. Table locks come in the following modes:

- **Row Share (RS)** – This lock, also called a subshare table lock (SS), indicates that the transaction holding the lock on the table has locked rows in the table and intends to update them. A row share lock is the least restrictive mode of table lock, offering the highest degree of concurrency for a table.
- **Row Exclusive Table Lock (RX)** – This lock, also called a subexclusive table lock (SX), generally indicates that the transaction holding the lock has updated table rows or issued SELECT ... FOR UPDATE. An SX lock allows other transactions to query, insert, update, delete, or lock rows concurrently in the same table. Therefore, SX locks allow multiple transactions to obtain simultaneous SX and subshare table locks for the same table.
- **Share Table Lock (S)** – A share table lock held by a transaction allows other transactions to query the table (without using SELECT ... FOR UPDATE), but updates are allowed only if a single transaction holds the share table lock. Because multiple transactions may hold a share table lock concurrently, holding this lock is not sufficient to ensure that a transaction can modify the table.

- **Share Row Exclusive Table Lock (SRX)** – This lock, also called a share-subexclusive table lock (SSX), is more restrictive than a share table lock. Only one transaction at a time can acquire an SSX lock on a given table. An SSX lock held by a transaction allows other transactions to query the table (except for SELECT ... FOR UPDATE) but not to update the table.
- **Exclusive Table Lock (X)** – This lock is the most restrictive, prohibiting other transactions from performing any type of DML statement or placing any type of lock on the table.

Deadlocks

When two or more users are waiting for data that is locked by the other user, this is known as a deadlock condition. If left alone, deadlocks can prevent transactions from continuing indefinitely. Oracle automatically detects deadlocked transactions and will resolve them by rolling back one of the statements creating in the deadlock. This will release one set of the conflicting row locks and allow the other transaction to complete. Deadlocks require a very specific set of circumstances and are very uncommon with Oracle's row-locking behavior. In fact, most commonly they occur when the default locking behavior has been explicitly overridden.

Database performance can be adversely affected by deadlocks, so Oracle provides some scripts and views that enable you to monitor locks. The utllockt.sql script displays sessions in the database waiting for locks, plus the locks that they are waiting for. You must run the catblock.sql script before running utllockt.sql. It will create the lock views needed to run utllockt.sql.

Monitoring Locks

There are several views that allow you to view locks being held by database sessions and/or sessions that are waiting on locked resources:

- **V$LOCK** – Lists the locks currently held by Oracle Database and outstanding requests for a lock or latch
- **DBA_BLOCKERS** – Displays a session if it is holding a lock on an object for which another session is waiting

- **DBA_WAITERS** – Displays a session if it is waiting for a locked object
- **DBA_DDL_LOCKS** – Lists all DDL locks held in the database and all outstanding requests for a DDL lock
- **DBA_DML_LOCKS** – Lists all DML locks held in the database and all outstanding requests for a DML lock
- **DBA_LOCK** – Lists all locks or latches held in the database and all outstanding requests for a lock or latch
- **DBA_LOCK_INTERNAL** – Displays a row for each lock or latch that is being held, and one row for each outstanding request for a lock or latch
- **V$LOCKED_OBJECT** – Lists all locks acquired by every transaction on the system

Resolving Lock Conflicts

If you find from the above views that one user session is blocking another (or several others) with an uncommitted transaction, the best method to resolve it is to ask the user to either commit or rollback the transaction holding the lock. This is both the fastest method and the one which has the least chance of creating other problems. If you kill the user's session, Oracle will have to roll back the transaction holding the lock. Rolling back a transaction normally takes longer than committing it. In addition, if the statement being rolled back was part of a series of transactions, rolling it back may introduce logical inconsistencies in the data the user was changing. Oracle will ensure that there are no inconsistencies from a granular data standpoint, but it's possible to introduce higher-level inconsistencies in the data. For this reason and others, killing sessions is generally a last resort for resolving locking conflicts.

One of the ways to locate blocking sessions is through the V$SESSION view. Issuing the following SQL statement will display all sessions that are blocking one or more other users and provide the data required to kill them:

```
SELECT  sid, serial#, username
FROM    v$session
WHERE   sid IN (SELECT blocking_session
                FROM    v$session);

SID SERIAL# USERNAME
-- ---- ----
 10   2127 OCPGURU
```

With that data, you can kill the blocking session:

```
ALTER SYSTEM KILL SESSION '10, 2127';
```

Managing Undo Data

Overview of Undo

Starting with Oracle 11G, automatic undo management is the default during database creation. DBCA will automatically create an auto-extending undo tablespace named UNDOTBS1. During startup, the database automatically uses the first available undo tablespace for undo records. If no undo tablespace is available, the instance will store undo records in the SYSTEM tablespace. This is not recommended. A warning will be written to the alert log file that the system is running without an undo tablespace. It's also possible for the database to run in manual undo management mode where undo space is managed through rollback segments. Rollback segments are not a test topic so this guide will focus on undo.

Whenever changes are made to the database, Oracle will simultaneously store the data that existed prior to the change. This is called undo or rollback data and is stored in the undo tablespace. When required, this information is used to undo changes to the database. Among other things, undo records are used to provide the following functionality:

- Roll back transactions when an implicit or explicit ROLLBACK is issued
- Recover after a failure
- Provide a read consistent view of the database
- Provide data from an earlier point in time using Oracle Flashback Query

When a ROLLBACK statement is issued, undo records are used to back out changes that were made to the database by the uncommitted transaction. If there is an abnormal shutdown of the database, during database recovery when the database is brought back up, the redo log will apply any data changes that did not make it to the datafiles. Then undo records are used to back out any uncommitted changes applied from the redo log to the datafiles. Read consistency is provided in the database by making use of the before image of the data that has been changed (but not committed). Users who access the data from rows that have been changed, but not committed will get their results back from the undo records rather than the changed information in the table record. With the undo records, multiple versions of the same data from different points in time, can exist in the database. The database can make use of the undo log to generate snapshots of data at different points in time.

Undo tablespaces can be associated with only a single instance, and each instance can have only a single undo tablespace writeable at a given time.

Transactions and undo data

At the start of a transaction, it is assigned to an undo segment. The transaction will use that segment until it is committed or rolled back – it cannot be shared among multiple undo segments. Undo segments, however, can service multiple transactions.

While a transaction is active, undo data is required to provide rollback or transaction recovery capabilities. At any time up until the transaction is committed, a user might issue an explicit rollback, or a connection problem might cause a session failure, or a wider problem might cause an abnormal instance shutdown. In any of these cases, the undo records will be needed to restore the database back to the condition that existed prior to the start of the transaction. Once a transaction has been committed, undo data is no longer needed for rollback or transaction recovery. However, it still has value for consistent read purposes. Queries must always be read-consistent as of the start time of the query. Since data might be changed after the start of long-running queries, undo information may be required for producing older images of data blocks. If a long-running transaction requires an older image of data to complete but the undo data has been overwritten before the query accesses it, the query will fail with an "ORA-1555: Snapshot too old" error. In addition, many of the Oracle Flashback features make use of undo information. Retaining old undo information for as long as possible is therefore desirable.

Managing undo

When automatic undo management is enabled, it has an undo retention period. This period is the minimum amount of time that the Database attempts to retain committed undo information before overwriting it. Any committed undo information that is older than retention period is considered to be expired, and a candidate to be overwritten. Committed undo information that is less than the retention period is unexpired and Oracle attempts to retain it for consistent read and Oracle Flashback operations. It is also possible to guarantee the retention period by enabling RETENTION GUARANTEE for the undo tablespace. If this is enabled, Oracle will never overwrite expired transactions that are more recent than the guaranteed period even if this means that new transactions will fail for lack of undo space.

Oracle will automatically tune the undo retention period based on the undo tablespace size and system activity. Alternately, you can explicitly set a minimum undo retention period with the UNDO_RETENTION initialization parameter. However, the UNDO_RETENTION parameter is ignored for a fixed size undo tablespace unless retention guarantee is enabled.

Implementing Oracle Database Security

Database security is generally broken into four main areas: user authentication, encryption, access control, and monitoring. A brief description of each and how Oracle implements them follows:

Authentication – The process by which a user provides credentials to the database. If the database determines that the credentials are invalid, the user is denied access to the database. If valid, the user is allowed access to the database and establishes a trusted relationship for further interactions. In addition, authentication leads to accountability by linking access and actions to a specific user account. Oracle can authenticate users in the database using a password, Kerberos ticket, PKI certificate or RADIUS-compliant devices. The authentication method is specified when the user account is created. Authentication for the database can also be provided by the operating system.

Encryption – The process by which data is transformed to an unreadable format. Encryption is sometimes required to meet regulatory compliance requirements. The data is transformed through the use of a secret key and an encryption algorithm. It's possible to use network encryption, where the data is encrypted as it travels across the network between. This prevents an intruder from using a network packet sniffer to capture information as it travels on the network. Alternately, Oracle Advanced Security transparent data encryption automatically encrypts data before it is inserted into a table column and decrypts it when the data is selected. This protects data in the table (but does not provide protection against sniffers).

Access Control – The process by which access to sensitive data is protected. Beyond the standard privileges built into the database, Oracle provides some specialized options to control access to data. Oracle Database Vault is a security option that restricts privileged user access to application data. Oracle Database Vault addresses common security problems such as protecting against insider threats (such as the DBA having complete access to the database). Virtual Private Database (VPD) allows for security to be provided at the row and column level. Oracle Label Security (OLS) is a security option that enables you to assign data classification and control access using security labels.

Monitoring – The process by which access to sensitive information is watched and logged. Database auditing is the monitoring and recording of selected user database actions. Standard auditing monitors SQL statements, privileges, schemas, objects, and more. Fine-grained auditing can be used to monitor specific database activities. Oracle Audit Vault and Oracle Enterprise Manager both have capabilities to administer database auditing.

Database Security and Principle of Least Privilege

The principle of least privilege means that users should be given the fewest privileges necessary to perform their jobs. Providing the fewest privileges possible minimizes the danger of inadvertent or malicious unauthorized activities. On the front-end, following this rule is definitely more work. For example, a given user might require twenty privileges to do their job. They won't know which privileges they need, and you as the DBA won't be positive either. You will probably have to grant them a set of privileges, have them test and report errors, then grant some more and retest, etc. It would be much easier to simply grant the user the DBA role or system privileges that they don't really require. Either would also be a very dangerous thing to do and might well create more work later if those privileges are misused. Oracle's recommendations on the principle of least privilege are:

- Do not provide database users or roles more privileges than are necessary.
- Restrict the number of SYSTEM and OBJECT privileges granted to database users.
- Restrict the number of people who are allowed to make SYS-privileged connections to the database.
- Restrict the number of users who are granted the ANY privileges.
- Restrict the number of users who are allowed to perform actions that create, modify, or drop database objects.
- Limit granting the CREATE ANY EDITION and DROP ANY EDITION privileges.
- Restrict the CREATE ANY JOB, BECOME USER, EXP_FULL_DATABASE, and IMP_FULL_DATABASE privileges.
- Restrict library-related privileges to trusted users only.

- Grant only the minimum required privileges to PUBLIC. Verify that the privileges it has are needed and revoke any that are not.
- Do not allow non-administrative users access to objects owned by the SYS schema.
- Only grant the EXECUTE privilege on the DBMS_RANDOM PL/SQL package to trusted users.
- Restrict permissions on run-time facilities.
- Use Access Control Lists (ACL) to control access to UTL_SMTP, UTL_TCP, UTL_HTTP, and UTL_FILE.

There are several other actions beyond the above that will provide for a more secure database environment.

- **Root** – The root account in Linux and the Administrator account in Windows have effectively unlimited privileges at the operating system level. In the hands of malicious or misguided users, they can do enormous damage to your database. The password to admin accounts should be complicated and the number of people given access very limited.
- **OS Accounts** – The number of operating system accounts created should be kept to the minimum possible. Every additional account provides another door through which an attacker can infiltrate your system. In most applications, there is no need for users to have an account on the database server.
- **Database Accounts** – As with operating system accounts, database accounts should be created only where necessary. If application interfaces connect via a shared account (for example Application Express connects via APEX_PUBLIC_USER), then users of a database may not require a database login. Reducing the number of accounts not only increases security but reduces administrative overhead.
- **SYSDBA / SYSOPER** – These two roles have considerable power over the database. As with the root OS account, you should grant this access to the smallest number of people that is feasible. Passwords for accounts with these roles should be complex and of mixed case.
- **Software** – Every application installed on the database server consumes space and requires memory when run. With few exceptions they will also require patches and upgrades, and may

have security holes that can be exploited. Install only the software required for your system.

- **Services** – If your database server is running an ftp server, a VNC server or other such remote access applications, they can be used as a means to enter your system. You should activate only services that are required and close any ports in your firewall for services that you do not use.

Work with Standard Database Auditing

Oracle's standard auditing feature monitors and records of selected user database actions. Auditing is performed on actions from both database users and non-database users. Standard auditing can be based on individual actions, such as SQL statements executed or on the use of specific system or object privileges. It's possible to audit both successful and failed attempts to perform activities. Oracle's auditing feature must be enabled and configured for the needs of a given database and actions will be recorded either in the data dictionary or in operating system files. Auditing is effective for enforcing strong internal controls.

Auditing is typically used to perform the following activities:
- Enable accountability for actions.
- Deter users or intruders from inappropriate actions.
- Investigate suspicious activity.
- Notify an auditor of unauthorized actions.
- Monitor and gather data about specific database activities.
- Detect problems with an authorization or access control.
- Address auditing requirements for regulatory compliance.

Standard auditing is enabled by setting the AUDIT_TRAIL initialization parameter. The valid options for this parameter are:

- **DB** – Directs audit records to the database audit trail, except for mandatory and SYS audit records, which are always written to the operating system audit trail. DB is the default setting for the AUDIT_TRAIL parameter.
- **DB, EXTENDED** – Same as DB, but also populates the SQL bind and SQL text CLOB-type columns of the SYS.AUD$ table with the SQL statement used in the action that was audited when available.

- **OS** – Directs all audit records to an operating system file. The AUDIT_FILE_DEST parameter determines the location of the file.
- **XML** – Writes to the operating system audit record file in XML format. The XML AUDIT_TRAIL value does not affect the syslog audit file. These records will always be in text format.
- **XML, EXTENDED** – Behaves the same as AUDIT_TRAIL=XML, but also includes SQL text and SQL bind information in the operating system XML audit files.
- **NONE** – Disables standard auditing.

The standard database audit trail is written to the SYS.AUD$ table and the fine-grained audit trail is written to SYS.FGA_LOG$. Audit records can only be deleted by someone who has connected with administrator privileges. Administrators must also be audited for unauthorized use. If the initialization parameter O7_DICTIONARY_ACCESSIBILITY is set to FALSE (the default), only SYSDBA users can perform DML on the SYS.AUD$ and SYS.FGA_LOG$ tables. Oracle Database Vault and Oracle Label Security can be used to add further protections if you have licenses for those products.

Certain database-related operations are always written to the operating system audit files. The actions of any user logged in with SYSDBA or SYSOPER are audited in this fashion. This is called mandatory auditing and will occur even if you have not enabled the database audit trail. The operating system files are in the $ORACLE_BASE/admin/$ORACLE_SID/adump directory by default.

Mandatory auditing includes the following operations:

- Database startup.
- SYSDBA and SYSOPER logins.
- Database shutdown.

Mandatory auditing can be supplemented with SYSDBA auditing by setting the initialization parameter AUDIT_SYS_OPERATIONS to TRUE. When enabled, top-level operations issued by users who have connected using the SYSDBA or SYSOPER privilege will be written to the operating system audit trail. The SQL text will be written to the ACTION field in the operating system audit trail record. This is more secure than auditing to the database tables because these users can alter those tables.

Fine-grained auditing (FGA) extends the capabilities of standard auditing. FGA allows for the definition of specific conditions that will trigger an audit record. This allows for granular auditing of queries, and DML operations. Whereas standard auditing could record if a SELECT operation was performed against a table, fine-grained auditing could be set if a SELECT against a table was performed at a given time or accessed a given column or a particular set of rows. Fine Grained Auditing therefore allows for much more focused auditing with less 'noise' from false hits.

Audit Views

There are a number of views with information about audit activity in the database. The following three views allow you to view the audit records stored in the database tables:

- **DBA_AUDIT_TRAIL** – Lists all standard audit trail entries in the AUD$ table.
- **DBA_FGA_AUDIT_TRAIL** – Lists audit trail records for fine-grained auditing.
- **DBA_COMMON_AUDIT_TRAIL** – Combines standard and fine-grained audit log records.

Database Maintenance

Historically, the tasks to be performed to maintain an Oracle database consumed significant amounts of time. In recent releases, Oracle has automated a number of common maintenance tasks previously performed manually. These automated maintenance tasks are typically scheduled to run after working hours or on weekends when the system load is light. The administrator can determine which maintenance tasks run, when they run and what resource allocations should be allotted to them. Automated maintenance tasks run in predefined time intervals called maintenance windows. Administrators should customize maintenance windows to match the resource usage patterns of your database so that they occur during periods of low activity. Alternately, it is possible to disable certain default windows from running or create custom maintenance windows.

The predefined maintenance windows are:

- **MONDAY_WINDOW** – Starts at 10 p.m. on Monday and ends at 2 a.m.
- **TUESDAY_WINDOW** – Starts at 10 p.m. on Tuesday and ends at 2 a.m.
- **WEDNESDAY_WINDOW** – Starts at 10 p.m. on Wednesday and ends at 2 a.m.
- **THURSDAY_WINDOW** – Starts at 10 p.m. on Thursday and ends at 2 a.m.
- **FRIDAY_WINDOW** – Starts at 10 p.m. on Friday and ends at 2 a.m.
- **SATURDAY_WINDOW** – Starts at 6 a.m. on Saturday and is 20 hours long.
- **SUNDAY_WINDOW** – Starts at 6 a.m. on Sunday and is 20 hours long.

There are three predefined automated maintenance tasks:

- **Automatic Optimizer Statistics Collection** -- Collects optimizer statistics for all schema objects in the database for which there are none or only stale statistics.

- **Automatic Segment Advisor** – Identifies segments that have space available for reclamation, and makes defragmentation recommendations.
- **Automatic SQL Tuning Advisor** – Examines the performance of high-load SQL statements, and makes tuning recommendations.

The activities performed by the automatic tasks and information returned shifts more of the maintenance to a proactive level – preventing problems from occurring. However, not every problem can or will be detected and prevented by automated tasks. These may generate errors that require a reactive response. The Oracle server will generate alerts and other diagnostic information when it detects a problem. The Automatic Diagnostic Repository works to collect this diagnostic information in a single location for easy access.

Use and manage optimizer statistics

The purpose of the Oracle optimizer is to determine the most efficient way to execute a SQL statement. Previously known as the Cost-Based Optimizer (to distinguish it from the legacy Rule-Based Optimizer), the optimizer is now referred to as either the query optimizer or the Automatic Tuning Advisor, depending on whether it is being run in normal mode or tuning mode. The two modes are described below:

- **Normal mode** – The optimizer compiles the SQL and generates an execution plan. This mode generates a reasonable plan for the vast majority of SQL statements. When running in normal mode, the output of the optimizer is an execution plan and is generally returned within a fraction of a second.

- **Tuning mode** – In this mode additional analysis is performed in an attempt to improve the plan produced in normal mode. The output from the optimizer is a set of actions for producing a significantly better plan. When running in tuning mode, the optimizer is known as the Automatic Tuning Optimizer.

SQL statements can be executed in multiple fashions, such as full table scans, index scans, nested loops, and hash joins. When selecting among potential execution plans, the optimizer considers many factors related to the objects and the conditions in the query. The specific method chosen can greatly affect execution time. When a SQL statement is submitted to the database, the optimizer performs the following steps:

1. Generates a set of potential plans for the SQL statement.
2. Estimates the cost of each plan based on statistics in the data dictionary.
3. Compares the plans and chooses the one with the lowest cost.

The statistics evaluated by the optimizer include information on the data distribution and storage characteristics of the tables and indexes accessed by the statement. The optimizer calculates the cost of access paths and join orders based on use of resources such as I/O, CPU, and memory. The sum of the costs for the individual actions for a given plan becomes the plan cost. Serial plans with higher costs take longer to execute than those with smaller costs. For plans executed in parallel, resource use is not directly related to elapsed time. The output from the optimizer is an execution plan that describes the optimum combination of steps to execute the SQL statement.

Optimizer Statistics

Statistics provide details about the database and the objects in it. The optimizer uses these statistics to calculate the optimum execution plan for each SQL statement. Optimizer statistics include the following:

- **Table statistics** – These include number of rows and blocks and the average row length.
- **Column statistics** – These include the number of distinct values, the number of nulls, the data distribution, and extended statistics.
- **Index statistics** – These include the number of leaf blocks, the number of levels, and the clustering factor.
- **System statistics** – These include I/O and CPU performance and utilization.

Optimizer statistics are stored in the database and can be accessed using data dictionary views. Statistics must be updated regularly in order for them to accurately describe the objects they represent. One of the automated maintenance tasks regularly updates database statistics for tables with absent or stale statistics to prevent them from becoming inaccurate. Automatic optimizer statistics collection calls the

GATHER_DATABASE_STATS_JOB_PROC procedure in the DBMS_STATS package. It prioritizes database objects that require statistics, so that objects that most need updated statistics are processed first, before the maintenance window closes. Automatic optimizer statistics collection runs as part of the automated maintenance tasks infrastructure (known as AutoTask) and is enabled by default to run in all predefined maintenance windows. If automatic statistics collection is disabled, it can be enabled using the ENABLE procedure in the DBMS_AUTO_TASK_ADMIN package:

```
BEGIN
DBMS_AUTO_TASK_ADMIN.ENABLE(
client_name => 'auto optimizer stats collection',
operation => NULL, window_name => NULL);
END;
/
```

Conversely, it can be disabled using the DISABLE procedure in the DBMS_AUTO_TASK_ADMIN package:

```
BEGIN
DBMS_AUTO_TASK_ADMIN.DISABLE(
client_name => 'auto optimizer stats collection',
operation => NULL, window_name => NULL);
END;
/
```

Use and Manage Automatic Workload Repository (AWR)

The Automatic Workload Repository (AWR) collects, processes, and maintains performance statistics about the database. This data is stored both in memory and in the database. The information collected is used to proactively detect problems and tune the database. The statistics collected include:

- Object statistics that determine both access and usage statistics of database segments
- Time model statistics based on time usage for activities
- Some of the system and session statistics collected in the V$SYSSTAT and V$SESSTAT views
- SQL statements that are producing the highest load on the system
- ASH statistics, representing the history of recent sessions activity

Statistics gathering by AWR is controlled by the STATISTICS_LEVEL initialization parameter. The STATISTICS_LEVEL parameter should be set to TYPICAL (the default) or ALL to enable statistics gathering by the AWR. If the STATISTICS_LEVEL parameter is set to BASIC, it disables many database features, including the AWR.

The values of the STATISTICS_LEVEL parameter are:

- **BASIC** – Disables AWR statistics collection. This also disables automatic daily analysis and alerts based on ADDM findings.
- **TYPICAL** – This is the default and automatically gathers the statistics required for Oracle's self-management and tuning capabilities. The daily analysis tasks are run during the maintenance windows.
- **ALL** – This option collects all possible statistics. It creates more overhead than is advisable for normal usage, but is useful for brief periods if actively performing SQL tuning.

Important aspects of AWR include:

- **Snapshot** – This is a set of historical data for a specific time period. The ADDM tool works by comparing metrics between multiple snapshots. By default, snapshots of the performance data are generated once every hour and retain eight days of statistics in the workload repository. The data in the snapshot interval is then analyzed by the Automatic Database Diagnostic Monitor (ADDM).
- **Baseline** – Contains performance data from a specific time period that is preserved indefinitely. They are used to provide a comparison with other similar workload periods when performance problems occur. The snapshots that make up a baseline are excluded from the automatic AWR purging.
- **Fixed Baseline** – These are made of a fixed, contiguous time period in the past. A fixed baseline should represent the system operating at an optimal level. Fixed baselines can be compared with other baselines captured during periods of poor performance to analyze performance degradation.
- **Moving Window Baseline** – Corresponds to all AWR data that exists within the AWR retention period. Moving window baselines are used in conjunction with adaptive thresholds. The entire AWR

retention period is used to compute metric threshold values. The default retention period is 8 days. Adaptive thresholds ideally should use a larger moving window to accurately compute threshold values.

- **Baseline Template** – Baselines for a contiguous time period in the future are created using baseline templates. It's possible to use a single baseline template to create a baseline for a single time period in the future. Alternately, you can use a repeating baseline template to create and drop baselines based on a repeating time schedule.

Use advisory framework

The Oracle Advisory Framework contains several different server components that provide information regarding resource utilization and performance. The core of the advisory framework is the Automatic Database Diagnostic Monitor (ADDM). ADDM makes use of snapshot data collected by AWR to perform analysis of the entire database. It can identify problems and their potential cause and often generates recommendations for resolving them. It also has the ability to call on other advisors. ADDM runs automatically in the background process MMON whenever a snapshot is taken and analyzes the statistics collected between the last two snapshots. ADDM identifies areas of the Database that are consuming the most time. The results of the ADDM analysis are written back to the workload repository for further use.

SQL Tuning Advisor

This advisor uses one or more SQL statements as an input and generates tuning recommendations, plus the reasoning behind each recommendation and the expected benefit. The advisor might suggest collecting statistics, creating new indexes, creating a SQL Profile, or restructuring the SQL statement itself. You can choose to accept the recommendations or not. SQL Tuning Advisor is known as the Automatic SQL Tuning Advisor when run during the system maintenance windows. By default the Automatic SQL Tuning Advisor runs nightly for at most one hour in the default maintenance windows and tunes high-load SQL statements from the AWR.

During automatic SQL tuning the advisor performs the following steps:

1. Identifies candidates in the AWR for tuning.
2. Tunes each SQL statement individually by calling SQL Tuning Advisor.
3. If a SQL profile is recommended, it is tested by executing the SQL statement with the profile.
4. A SQL profile will be implemented if it provides a threefold performance improvement.

For databases using SQL plan management, the database adds a new plan baseline when creating the profile if a SQL plan baseline for the SQL statement exists. This allows the optimizer to use the new plan immediately. The automatic SQL tuning report allows you to view the results any time during or after the automatic SQL tuning process. It provides details of the statements analyzed, the recommendations generated, and the SQL profiles that were implemented.

SQL Access Advisor

Databases that are subject to complex and data-intensive queries should make use of indexes, partitions, and materialized views in order to achieve optimum performance. The SQL Access Advisor is designed to recommend the proper set of indexes, partitions, materialized views, and materialized view logs for a given workload. Used properly, each of these can result in significant performance improvements in data retrieval. They each come with their own maintenance and space requirements and so must not be implemented without a valid reason. SQL Access Advisor uses statistics about tables and indexes to make recommendations. If a given table has no statistics, queries referencing it are marked as invalid in the workload and no Access Advisor recommendations will be made for them.

- Index recommendations include bitmap, function-based, and B-tree indexes.
- View recommendations include fast refreshable and full refreshable Materialized Views.
- It can recommend partitioning an existing unpartitioned base table to improve performance or new indexes or materialized views that are partitioned.

Data Recovery Advisor

The Data Recovery Advisor (DRA) tool diagnoses data failures, provides repair options, and executes repairs. The Data Recovery Advisor has the capability to repair corruptions in data blocks, the data dictionary, undo blocks, and more. It is integrated with database health checks, OEM, and RMAN to provide the following functions:

- Display data corruption problems.
- Determine the severity of each problem (critical, high priority, low priority).
- Describe the impact of a problem.
- Recommend repair options.
- Check the feasibility of a customer-chosen option.
- Automate the repair process.

SQL Repair Advisor

The SQL Repair Advisor is only used when a SQL statement fails with a critical error. The advisor will analyze the failing statement and may be able to recommend a patch to repair it. If implemented, the applied SQL patch causes the query optimizer to choose an alternate execution plan for future executions. In many ways the patch acts like a SQL Profile. The SQL Repair Advisor never changes the SQL statement itself and it is used to repair failing SQL, not to tune functional SQL.

Undo Advisor

Automatic tuning of undo retention generally works better when using a fixed-size undo tablespace. The Undo Advisor is designed to help estimate needed capacity for a fixed-size undo tablespace. The Undo Advisor uses AWR data for its analysis. You should not attempt to use the Undo Advisor before the AWR has adequate workload statistics available. In order to use the Undo Advisor, you first estimate the following:

- The length of longest running query expected for your database
- The longest flashback period that you need for Oracle Flashback operations

You must use the larger of these two values as input to the Undo Advisor. The Undo Advisor returns a recommended size for your undo tablespace, but will not alter the size itself. You can use the Undo Advisor by creating an undo advisor task through the advisor framework. The output and recommendations can be seen in the Automatic Database Diagnostic Monitor in Enterprise Manager. The information is also available in the DBA_ADVISOR_* data dictionary views.

Segment Advisor

The task of the Segment Advisor is to identify segments with space that can be reclaimed. Segment Advisor examines usage and growth metrics in the AWR, and also samples data in the segments themselves.

The Segment Advisor runs as an automated maintenance task where it is known as the Automatic Segment Advisor. It can generate the following types of advice:

- If an object has a significant amount of free space, it recommends online segment shrink.
- If a table that is not eligible for shrinking has a significant amount of free space, the Advisor recommends online table redefinition.
- If a table would benefit from compression with the OLTP compression method, the Advisor makes a recommendation to use it.
- If a table has row chaining above a certain threshold, the Advisor generates a record to that effect.

The Automatic Segment Advisor selects the following objects to analyze:

- Tablespaces that have exceeded a critical or warning space threshold
- Segments that have the most activity
- Segments that have the highest growth rate

The Segment Advisor will also investigate tables that are at least 10 megabytes when they have at least three indexes. It determines the space that could be saved by using the OLTP compression method on these tables. Any objects that are selected for processing but are not evaluated by the time the window closes are evaluated on the subsequent run of the advisor. It's not possible to alter which tablespaces and segments will be evaluated by the advisor. You can only enable or disable the Automatic Segment Advisor task or change the resource utilization. The advisor can be run manually with Oracle Enterprise manager or via PL/SQL.

There are three levels of advice provided by the Segment Advisor:

- **Segment** – This level generates advice for a single segment.
- **Object** – This level will generate advice for an entire object. For example, with a partitioned table, the segment level would generate advice on one partition, but object level would generate advice for the entire table.
- **Tablespace** – This level will generate advice for every segment in a tablespace.

MTTR Advisor

The MTTR Advisor is used to assist you in setting the value of the initialization parameter FAST_START_MTTR_TARGET. When this parameter is set, the advisor can evaluate the effect of different values on system performance compared to the current setting. In addition to the FAST_START_MTTR_TARGET parameter, the STATISTICS_LEVEL parameter must be set to TYPICAL or ALL in order for the MTTR Advisor to be enabled. Once a typical workload has been run on the database with these parameters set, you can view advice regarding setting the MTTR target in the V$MTTR_TARGET_ADVICE view. The view will contain advice about the effects of several FAST_START_MTTR_TARGET settings for your database.

Manage Alerts and Thresholds

Alerts

The background processes and servers that make up an Oracle instance each have their own trace file. If a process detects an error condition, it will dump information about the error out to its particular trace file. Some of the trace file information is intended for the use of the database administrator, and the remainder is for Oracle Support. In addition to the trace files, there is the database alert log. It contains a chronological list of messages and errors from the database. Some of the messages recorded in the alert log include:

- Initialization parameters with non-default values at instance startup.
- All occurrences of the following errors: internal (ORA-600), block corruption (ORA-1578), and deadlock (ORA-60).
- Many administrative commands, including CREATE, ALTER, and DROP DDL statements as well as STARTUP and SHUTDOWN.

With Oracle 11G, the alert log is maintained simultaneously in two versions: an XML-formatted file and a text-formatted file. Either version of the alert log can be viewed with a text editor. Alternately, the ADRCI utility can be used to view the XML-formatted version with the XML tags removed. One of the duties of a DBA is to periodically check the alert log and trace files to see if the server or any background processes have encountered errors. The alert log and trace files are written out to directories that are part of the Automatic Diagnostic Repository. Trace file names generally include the name of the process that writes to the file, such as MMON and LGWR. The MAX_DUMP_FILE_SIZE can be used to limit the file size of trace files to the specified number of operating system blocks. It is not possible to limit the size of the alert log. You must periodically delete the file to control the size. This can be done while the instance is running. Generally, you should create an archive copy prior to deleting the file.

Any time a critical error occurs, one or more trace files will be written on behalf of the involved server processes. In addition, if the SQL_TRACE initialization parameter is set to TRUE, the SQL trace facility will generate performance statistics for all SQL statements processed by the instance. These traces are then written to the ADR. Alternately, SQL tracing can be enabled at a session level by issuing the command ALTER SESSION SET SQL_TRACE. The DBMS_SESSION and DBMS_MONITOR packages can be used to control SQL tracing for a session.

Adaptive Thresholds

It's possible to monitor database performance continuously using adaptive thresholds. The DBA can set warning and critical alert thresholds for numerous system metrics. These thresholds are created using statistics derived from metrics captured in the moving window baseline. The statistics for the moving window metrics are recomputed weekly and may result in new thresholds if the system performance changes. Adaptive thresholds can detect different workload patterns of the database, such as OLTP activity during the day, batch processing at night, and backups on the weekend. Once detected, it will automatically set different threshold values for the performance pattern detected.

There are two types of adaptive thresholds:

Percentage of maximum – The threshold value is computed as a percentage multiple of the maximum value observed for the data in the moving window baseline (for example 95% of the maximum value observed).

Significance level – The threshold value is set to a percentile representing how unusual it is to observe values above the threshold. It is set to one of the following percentiles:
- **High (.95)** – Only 5 in 100 observations are expected to exceed this value.
- **Very High (.99)** – Only 1 in 100 observations are expected to exceed this value.
- **Severe (.999)** – Only 1 in 1,000 observations are expected to exceed this value.
- **Extreme (.9999)** – Only 1 in 10,000 observations are expected to exceed this value.

Performance Management

Use Automatic Memory Management

Tuning the various memory pools of an Oracle server used to be a very manual process and one that involved a fair amount of guesswork. Over the past several releases, Oracle has adding increasing amounts of automation to this process. With 11G, it's possible to set a single parameter that allows the Database instance to automatically manage all of the memory pools. The process to do this is to set the MEMORY_TARGET parameter to a target memory size. The Oracle instance will grab this much memory on startup. Optionally you can specify a maximum memory size with the MEMORY_MAX_TARGET initialization parameter. The MEMORY_TARGET initialization parameter is dynamic and can be changed without restarting the database. However, the MEMORY_MAX_TARGET is not dynamic and requires a shutdown to change. It serves as an upper limit on the value assigned to the MEMORY_TARGET parameter so that you cannot accidentally set it too high.

When using Automatic memory management, the instance distributes memory between the SGA and PGA automatically. The instance dynamically redistributes memory between the two as memory requirements change. Databases created with DBCA using the basic installation option will have automatic memory management enabled by default. If a database is not currently using Automatic Memory Management, you can enable it using the following commands:

```
ALTER SYSTEM SET MEMORY_TARGET = nM;
ALTER SYSTEM SET SGA_TARGET = 0;
ALTER SYSTEM SET PGA_AGGREGATE_TARGET = 0;
```

Optionally you can issue the following command:

```
ALTER SYSTEM SET MEMORY_MAX_TARGET = nM SCOPE = SPFILE;
```

The relationships between the four parameters utilized by Automatic Memory Management are:

- **memory_target** – When MEMORY_TARGET is set, the database will allocate this much memory on startup, by default granting 60% to the SGA and 40% to the PGA. Over time, as the database runs, it will redistribute memory as needed between the system global area (SGA) and the instance program global area (instance PGA). If MEMORY_TARGET is not set, automatic memory management is not enabled, even if you have set a value for MEMORY_MAX_TARGET.
- **memory_max_target** – When set, this determines the maximum amount of memory that Oracle will grab from the OS for the SGA and PGA. If this value is not set, it will default to the MEMORY_TARGET value.
- **sga_target** – This value is not required if using automatic memory management. If this value is set and MEMORY_TARGET is also set, then the value of SGA_TARGET becomes the minimum amount of memory allocated to the SGA by automatic memory management.
- **pga_aggregate_target** – This value is not required if using automatic memory management. If this value is set and MEMORY_TARGET is also set, then the value of PGA_AGGREGATE_TARGET becomes the minimum amount of memory allocated to the PGA by automatic memory management.

Use Memory Advisors

The Automatic Memory Management feature of Oracle 11G performs all memory adjustments without human intervention. There is no need for an advisor to suggest adjustments of that sort. However, these adjustments are made within the boundaries of the memory you have assigned to Oracle. The Memory Advisor can make recommendations that you increase the total amount of memory assigned to Oracle if it determines that memory is impacting performance. In addition, the memory advisors can perform an analysis of:

- The performance benefits of adding physical memory to the database
- The performance impact of reducing the amount of physical memory available to the database

It is also possible to get memory sizing advice for:

- Setting the target amount of memory to allocate to the Oracle instance when using automatic memory management.
- Configuring the target sizes of the SGA and instance PGA when using automatic shared memory management.
- Sizing the shared pool, buffer cache, and instance PGA when using manual shared memory management.

The Memory Advisors are accessed via Oracle Enterprise Manager. You can view more about using them in the *Oracle Database 2 Day + Performance Tuning Guide*.

Troubleshoot invalid and unusable objects

Objects in the Oracle database will sometimes have references to other objects. Views reference the table or tables that they query. PL/SQL procedures may reference tables or other procedures. Any object that has such a dependency is called a dependent object. Any object with such a reference against it is called a referenced object. If some event occurs such that the dependent object cannot resolve any or all of its references, it will be marked invalid. Oracle tracks all such dependencies in the database. If a change is made to a referenced object that might affect a dependent object, the dependent object is marked invalid. The following query will display any invalid objects in the database:

```
SELECT object_name, object_type
FROM   dba_objects
WHERE  status = 'INVALID';
```

If a procedure, function or package is invalidated, it can cause exceptions in other sessions that are concurrently executing it. Any time an object has been marked as invalid, it must be recompiled against referenced objects before it can be used. Oracle will automatically perform a recompile the first time the invalid dependent object is referenced. Alternately, you can force recompilation on a schema object using the appropriate SQL statement with the COMPILE clause. When there is a large number of invalid objects, the UTL_RECOMP package can be used to perform a mass recompilation.

Some of the rules for the invalidation of schema objects are:

- When object becomes invalid for any reason, any objects that depend on it are simultaneously invalidated as well.
- If object privileges are revoked on a schema object, the invalidation cascades to dependent objects.
- The database tracks the elements of the referenced object that are involved in the dependency. For example, in a view that selects a subset of columns of a table, only the selected columns define the dependency. If the SELECTed columns of the table are altered, the view becomes invalid. However, if only non-referenced columns are changed, or dropped, the view is unaffected.

Recompiling Invalid Objects

You can recompile a single object using an ALTER statement. To recompile package body ocp_main, you would execute the following:

```
ALTER PACKAGE ocp_main COMPILE REUSE SETTINGS;
```

Alternately, you can use the UTL_RECOMP package to assist in object revalidation. The package has the RECOMP_SERIAL and RECOMP_PARALLEL procedures, which recompile objects in serial or parallel (employing multiple CPUs) respectively. If the procedures are passed a schema name then they will recompile the specified schema. When no schema name is passed, they will recompile all invalid objects in the database. The following example will revalidate all invalid objects in the database, in parallel and in dependency order:

```
BEGIN
  utl_recomp.recomp_parallel();
END;
```

You can also use the utlrp script to recompile all objects in the database. This should be run when connected to the database as SYSDBA:

```
@[ORACLE_HOME]/rdbms/admin/utlrp
```

Unusable indexes

When an index has been marked as unusable, it is not maintained during DML operations and it is ignored by the optimizer. A DBA might mark an index as unusable in order to improve performance during a bulk load. With the index marked as unusable, the overhead of maintaining the index during the load operation is eliminated. Once the load operation has been completed, rather than having to recreate the index, it can simply be rebuilt using the ALTER INDEX command with the REBUILD clause. In some cases an index may be marked unusable by the database if a failure occurs during an index operation. It can also happen if a table is moved (because the ROWIDs of the table rows will change). If an index or index partition has been marked unusable, it must be rebuilt or re-created before it can be used. Truncating the indexed table will also make an unusable index valid. When an existing index is marked as unusable, its index segment is dropped (starting with 11.2).

When the SKIP_UNUSABLE_INDEXES initialization parameter is TRUE (the default), unusable indexes exhibit the following behavior:

- DML statements against the table proceed, but unusable indexes are not maintained.
- DML statements terminate with an error if there are any unusable indexes that are used to enforce the UNIQUE constraint.
- For nonpartitioned indexes, the optimizer does not consider any unusable indexes when creating an access plan for SELECT statements. The only exception is when an index is explicitly specified with the INDEX() hint.
- For a partitioned index that contains one or more unusable partitions, the optimizer does not consider the index if it cannot determine at query compilation time if any of the index partitions can be pruned. The only exception is when an index is explicitly specified with the INDEX() hint.

When SKIP_UNUSABLE_INDEXES is FALSE, then:

- If any unusable indexes or index partitions are present, any DML statements that would cause those indexes or index partitions to be updated are terminated with an error.
- For SELECT statements, if an unusable index or unusable index partition is present but the optimizer does not choose to use it for the access plan, the statement proceeds. However, if the optimizer does choose to use the unusable index or unusable index partition, the statement terminates with an error.

Intelligent Infrastructure Enhancements

Use the Enterprise Manager Support Workbench

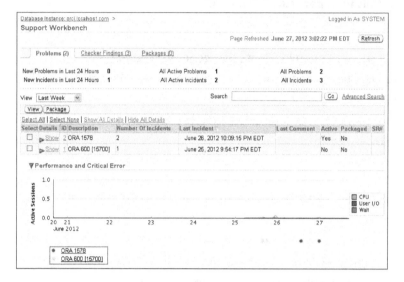

To access the Support Workbench home page:

1. From Oracle Enterprise Manager, access the Database Home page.
2. Perform one of the following actions:
   - In the Diagnostic Summary section, click the numeric link next to the Active Incidents label.
   - Click Software and Support at the top of the page. Under Support, click Support Workbench.

To view problems and incidents:

1. Select the time period to be displayed from the View list. Select "All" to view all problems.
2. Click the Show/Hide icon adjacent to the Performance and Critical Error section if it is hidden.

3. Under the Details column, click Show to display a list of all incidents for a problem.

To view details for a particular problem:

1. Select the problem, and then click View. The incidents subpage will show all open incidents that generated dumps.
2. To view both open and closed incidents, select All Incidents in the Status list.
3. To view details for an incident, select the incident, and then click View.

To view details for a particular incident:

From the Incident Details page:

1. Click Checker Findings to view checker findings for the incident.
2. To view available user actions for the incident, click Additional Diagnostics. These provide a way to gather additional diagnostics.

Managing Patches

After installation and on a regular basis, DBAs should download and install patches to the Oracle software. There are three varieties of patches produced by Oracle:

- **Interim patches** – These address individual software bugs and may or may not be needed at your installation.
- **Patch releases** – Also known as patch sets, these are collections of bug fixes that are applicable for all customers. Patch releases have release numbers.
- **Critical Patch Updates** – CPUs are the primary means of releasing security fixes for Oracle products to customers with valid support contracts.

Some patches can be installed while the database is running using either OPatch or the Enterprise Manager Patch Wizard (which uses opatch in the background). You can determine what patches are applicable to your system through the Patch Advisor in Enterprise Manager.

Online Patches

Prior to 11G, all patches contained .o (object) files and/or .a (archive) libraries. Installing them required a relink of the RDBMS binary and therefore meant the database had to be shut down before the patch could be applied. With 11G, some patches are available as online patches. These contain .so files, which are dynamic/shared libraries, and they do not require a relink of the RDBMS binary. Because a relink is not needed, online patches can be applied or rolled back while the database instance is running. This simplifies administration, because no downtime is needed. It also means that installing or de-installing Online Patches is faster – potentially taking just a few seconds. Online patches will be installed using the opatch utility.

The benefits of online patches include the following:
- No downtime is required
- They persist across shutdowns
- They allow rolling patches in RAC
- They have a fast installation

There are few downsides to online patches:
- They require more memory
- Online patching isn't available on all platforms
- Not all patches are available as hot patches

Backup and Recovery Concepts

Identify the types of failure that can occur in an Oracle database

There are a number of different problems that can affect the normal operation of an Oracle database or impair database I/O operations. However, the failures that require DBA intervention and data repair generally fall into one of three categories: user errors, application errors, and media failures.

- **User Errors** – These occur when data in your database is changed or deleted incorrectly through the actions of users. The root cause might be an error in application logic or a manual mistake. An example would be when a user drops a database table by mistake.
- **Application Errors** – It is possible for a software malfunction to corrupt data blocks. If this takes the form of a physical corruption (also known as a media corruption), the database does not recognize the block.
- **Media Failures** – In a media failure, a problem external to the database prevents it from reading from or writing to a database file while the instance is running. Common media failures include disk failures and the deletion of database files.

There are other failure classes. However, these do not typically result in the need for DBA intervention or media recovery:

- **Statement Failure** – If a SQL statement fails, all changes made by it will be automatically rolled back. The failure of a single SQL statement will not impact other statements in the transaction.
- **User Process Failure** – If a user session or process fails, PMON will automatically detect this and clean up after it. Any transactions

that were active at the time of the failure will be rolled back and all locks held will be released.

- **Instance Failure** – If the database instance fails or is shut down with the ABORT clause, the database will perform instance recovery on the next startup.

Describe ways to tune instance recovery

Instance and crash recovery is the automatic application of redo log records to data blocks after a crash or system failure. Any time an instance is shut down cleanly, changes that are in memory but have not been written to the data files are written to disk during the shutdown checkpoint. However, if a database is shutdown with the abort option, or a single instance database crashes or if all instances of an Oracle RAC configuration crash, then this checkpoint does not occur. In these cases, the Oracle Database will perform a crash recovery on the next startup. There are two steps to instance and crash recovery: cache recovery followed by transaction recovery. Because the database can be opened once cache recovery completes, improving the performance of this step increases availability.

- **Cache Recovery** – In the cache recovery step (also known as rolling forward), the Database applies all committed and uncommitted changes in the redo log files to the affected data blocks. The amount of work required for cache recovery is proportional to the rate of change for the database and the time between checkpoints.
- **Transaction Recovery** – Once all changes from the redo log are applied to the data files, any changes that were not committed at the time of the crash must be rolled back. In the transaction recovery step, the database uses rollback information to back out the uncommitted changes.

Periodically, Oracle Database records the highest system change number (SCN) for which all data blocks less than or equal to that SCN are known to be written out to the data files. This is called a checkpoint. If there is an instance failure, only redo records with changes above the last checkpoint SCN must be applied during recovery. The duration of cache recovery processing is determined by two factors: the number of data blocks that have changes at SCNs higher than the SCN of the checkpoint, and the number of log blocks that need to be read to find those changes. A database that checkpoints frequently will write dirty buffers to the data files more often. This will reduce cache recovery time in the event of an instance failure because fewer redo blocks will have to be applied to the datafiles. However, frequent checkpointing in a high-update system can reduce database performance.

Oracle's Fast-Start Fault Recovery feature is intended to reduce cache recovery time and make it predictable. It does this by limiting the number of dirty buffers and the number of redo records generated between the most recent redo record and the last checkpoint. This feature uses the Fast-Start checkpointing architecture instead of conventional event-driven checkpointing. Instead of the bulk writes used by conventional checkpointing, fast-start checkpointing occurs incrementally. Each DBWn process periodically writes buffers to disk to advance the checkpoint position. This eliminates the I/O spikes that occur with conventional checkpointing. The FAST_START_MTTR_TARGET initialization parameter enables Fast-Start Fault Recovery and simplifies the configuration of recovery time from instance or system failure. The parameter sets a target for the expected mean time to recover (MTTR). The value of parameter is the time (in seconds) that it should take to start up the instance and perform cache recovery. Once set, the database manages incremental checkpoints in an attempt to meet that target.

Identify the importance of checkpoints, redo log files, and archived log files

Redo Logs
The redo log is the single most crucial structure for recovery operations. A redo log consists of two or more pre-allocated files that store all changes made to the database as they occur. Every Oracle Database instance has an associated redo log for protection in case of an instance failure. The log files contain redo records. A redo record is a group of change vectors, each of which is a description of a change made to a single block in the database. A change made to a given table in the database will generate a redo record with change vectors for the data segment block for the table, the undo segment data block, and the transaction table of the undo segments. The information in redo entries can be used to reconstruct all changes made to the database, including the undo segments. Redo records can be written to a redo log file before the corresponding transaction has been committed. If the redo log buffer fills, or another database transaction is committed, LGWR flushes all of the entries in the redo log buffer to a redo log file. If necessary, the database can roll back any uncommitted changes. Committed changes will be written to the redo log before those changes are written to the data files. In the event of an instance failure, the redo logs are what ensure that committed database transactions are never lost.

Checkpoints
Periodically, all modified database buffers in the system global area are written to the datafiles by DBWn. This is known as a checkpoint. The checkpoint process is responsible for signaling DBWn at checkpoints and updating all the datafiles and control files of the database to indicate the most recent checkpoint. In the event of an instance failure, Oracle must know where to start when applying redo information to the datafiles. The SCN of the most recent checkpoint provides that starting point.

Archive Logs
An archived redo log file is a copy of one of the filled members of a redo log group. It includes the redo entries and the unique log sequence number of the identical member of the redo log group. Whereas redo logs are used for instance recovery, archive logs are used for media recovery. Instance recovery happens after a database crash or shutdown abort. The database files that were in use at the time of the crash are updated and

made consistent using redo logs. Media recovery occurs when one or more backup copies of database data files are used for recovery. In this case, the old files must have all changes applied to them from the time the backup was taken until the present date in order to be made current. This is media recovery and requires the use of archived redo logs.

Overview of fast recovery area

As of Oracle 11g release 2, the Flash Recovery Area has been renamed to the Fast Recovery Area. This was done to prevent it from being confused with the flashback database. The test might use either name to refer to this feature. The Fast Recovery Area is a location in which the database can store and manage files related to backup and recovery. The location is separate from the database area, where the current database files are located. The fast recovery area can contain control files, online redo logs, archived redo logs, flashback logs, and RMAN backups. Files in the recovery area are labeled as permanent or transient. Permanent files are active files used by the database instance – all others are transient. Transient files are generally deleted after they become obsolete or have been backed up to tape. Files placed in this location are maintained by Oracle Database and the generated file names are maintained in Oracle Managed Files (OMF) format.

You must specify the following initialization parameters to enable the Fast Recovery Area:

- **DB_RECOVERY_FILE_DEST** – Location of the Fast Recovery Area. This can be a directory, file system, or Automatic Storage Management (Oracle ASM) disk group.
  DB_RECOVERY_FILE_DEST_SIZE – Specifies the maximum total bytes to be used by the Fast Recovery Area. This initialization parameter must be specified before DB_RECOVERY_FILE_DEST is enabled.

These parameters cannot be enabled if you have set values for the parameters LOG_ARCHIVE_DEST and LOG_ARCHIVE_DUPLEX_DEST. You must disable those parameters before setting up the Fast Recovery Area. You can instead set values for the LOG_ARCHIVE_DEST_n parameters. The LOG_ARCHIVE_DEST_1 parameter is implicitly set to point to the Fast

Recovery Area if a local archiving location has not been configured and LOG_ARCHIVE_DEST_1 value has not been set.

Managing Space in the Fast Recovery Area

The database issues a warning alert when reclaimable space is less than 15% and a critical alert when reclaimable space is less than 3%. An entry is added to the alert log and to the DBA_OUTSTANDING_ALERTS table to warn the DBA of this condition. If not resolved, the database will consume space in the fast recovery area until there is no space left.

You can resolve low space issues in the Fast Recovery Area in several ways:

- Make more disk space available and increase DB_RECOVERY_FILE_DEST_SIZE.
- Move backups from the fast recovery area to tertiary storage such as tape. The BACKUP RECOVERY AREA command will back up all of your recovery area files to tape.
- Run DELETE for any files that have been removed with an operating system utility. The database is not aware of file removed by OS commands.
- Run the RMAN CROSSCHECK command to have RMAN recheck the contents of the fast recovery area and identify expired files, and then use the DELETE EXPIRED command to delete every expired backup from the RMAN repository.
- Delete any unnecessary guaranteed restore points.
- Review your backup retention policy and make it less restrictive.

Information about the Fast Recovery Area is stored in the V$RECOVERY_FILE_DEST dynamic view. In addition, the column IS_RECOVERY_DEST_FILE has been added to the following views: V$CONTROLFILE, V$LOGFILE, V$ARCHIVED_LOG, V$DATAFILE_COPY, V$BACKUP_PIECE and the RMAN tables. This column has a value of YES if a file of the corresponding kind has been created in the fast recovery area.

Configure ARCHIVELOG mode

In order to toggle the archiving mode of the database, use the ALTER DATABASE statement with the ARCHIVELOG or NOARCHIVELOG clause. You must be logged in to the database with administrator privileges in order to alter the archiving mode. The following steps will enable ARCHIVELOG on a database:

1. Shut down the database instance. The database must be closed and all associated instances shut down in order to switch the database archiving mode. It is also not possible to change the mode from ARCHIVELOG to NOARCHIVELOG if any datafiles need media recovery.
2. Edit the initialization parameter file. Add required parameters to specify the destinations for the archived redo log files.
3. Perform a STARTUP MOUNT on the database.
4. Change the database archiving mode by issuing ALTER DATABASE ARCHIVELOG. Then open the database for normal operations by issuing ALTER DATABASE OPEN.
5. Shut down the database.
6. Back up the database. Because changing the archiving mode updates the control file, you must back up all of your database files and control file. Previous backups are no longer usable.

Performing Database Backups

Create consistent database backups

A consistent backup is one that is created when the database is in a consistent state. A database is only in a consistent state while it is shut down. In addition, it must be shut down with the SHUTDOWN NORMAL, SHUTDOWN IMMEDIATE, or SHUTDOWN TRANSACTIONAL commands. A database that has been shut down using the ABORT keyword will be inconsistent. A consistent shutdown ensures that all redo has been applied to the datafiles and a checkpoint taken. If you mount a database in a consistent state and create a backup of it, then you can restore that backup later and open it without the need to perform any media recovery. Control files play a crucial role in database restore and recovery.

Databases that are running in NOARCHIVELOG mode can only be backed up when the database is closed and in a consistent state. The example below ensures the database is in the correct mode for a consistent, whole database backup. It then backs up the database.

```
SHUTDOWN IMMEDIATE;
STARTUP FORCE DBA;
SHUTDOWN IMMEDIATE;
STARTUP MOUNT;

BACKUP
INCREMENTAL LEVEL 0
MAXSETSIZE 10M
DATABASE
TAG 'FULL_BACKUP';

ALTER DATABASE OPEN;
```

When RMAN is used to back up the database, the oracle terminology is a server-managed backup. If a backup is taken through operating system commands or a third-party software, Oracle refers to it as a user-managed backup. Server-managed backups have several advantages over user-managed backups, including:

- RMAN only backs up used blocks, resulting in smaller backup files.
- Automation of backup and recovery through RMAN.
- Incremental backups that only contain data blocks changed since the previous backup.
- Built-in scripting language in RMAN for backup and recovery automation.

When the database is shut down cleanly, you can perform a user-managed backup of the database with an operating system utility. To make a consistent whole database backup using operating system commands:

1. If the database is open, then use SQL*Plus to shut down the database with the NORMAL, IMMEDIATE, or TRANSACTIONAL options.
2. Use an operating system utility to copy all data files and all control files specified by the CONTROL_FILES parameter of the initialization parameter file to a backup location. You should also back up the initialization parameter files. For example, you can back up the data files, control files, and archived logs to /u02/oradata/backup as follows:

```
cp $ORACLE_HOME/oradata/ocpdb/*.dbf
/u02/oradata/backup
cp $ORACLE_HOME/oradata/ocpdb/arch/*
/u02/oradata/backup/arch
```

3. Restart the database with the STARTUP command in SQL*Plus.

Back up your database without shutting it down

For a database running in ARCHIVELOG mode, it is possible to back the database up while it is open. The backup is called an inconsistent backup because redo is required during recovery to bring the database to a consistent state. It is also known as an ONLINE backup. So long as you have the archived redo logs required to recover the backup, open database backups are an effective way to protect the database. To back up the database and archived redo logs using the RMAN tool while the database is open:

1. Start RMAN and connect to a target database.
2. Run the BACKUP DATABASE command.

```
RMAN> BACKUP DATABASE PLUS ARCHIVELOG;
```

Online User-managed Backup

It is also possible to use operating system utilities to back up datafiles for an online database running in ARCHIVELOG mode. However, the process is considerably more complex than using RMAN. It is possible that an operating system utility might back up a data file at the same time that the database writer (DBWR) is updating the file. In this instance, the utility might read a block in a half-updated state. This type of logical corruption is known as a fractured block. If this backup was restored later, and a fractured block required recovery, the recovery would fail. For a user-managed online backup, datafiles must be placed into backup mode with the ALTER DATABASE or ALTER TABLESPACE statement with the BEGIN BACKUP clause. RMAN does not require backup mode because it knows the format of data blocks and is guaranteed not to back up fractured blocks.

Create incremental backups

The RMAN BACKUP INCREMENTAL command creates an incremental backup of a database. Incremental backups capture block-level changes to a database made after a previous incremental backup. Recovery with incremental backups is faster than using redo logs alone. There are three types of incremental backups:

- **Level 0** – This is the starting point for an incremental backup. It backs up all blocks that have ever been in use in the database and is identical in content to a full backup.
- **Level 1 Differential** – This backup contains only blocks changed since the most recent incremental backup. This is the default Level 1 backup.
- **Level 1 Cumulative** – This backup contains only blocks changed since the most recent level 0 backup.

When restoring incremental backups, RMAN uses the level 0 backup as the starting point. It then uses the level 1 backups to update changed blocks where possible to avoid reapplying changes from redo one at a time. If incremental backups are available, then RMAN uses them during recovery.

The following example creates a level 0 incremental backup to serve as a base for an incremental backup strategy:

```
BACKUP INCREMENTAL LEVEL 0 DATABASE;
```

The following example creates a level 1 cumulative incremental backup:

```
BACKUP INCREMENTAL LEVEL 1 CUMULATIVE DATABASE;
```

The following example creates a level 1 differential incremental backup:

```
BACKUP INCREMENTAL LEVEL 1 DATABASE;
```

Using an incrementally updated backup strategy allows you to benefit from the smaller footprint of differential backups, while minimizing down time if there is a failure that requires a database recovery. The RMAN incrementally updated backup strategy has the following main features:

- A level 0 data file copy is created as a base. This copy has either a system-defined or user-defined tag.
- Periodically, level 1 differential backups are created with the same tag as the level 0 data file copy.
- Periodically, the incremental backups are applied to the level 0 data file copy. Because the data file copy has been updated with more recent changes, it now requires less media recovery.

Automate database backups

Control File and Server Parameter File Autobackups

When performing a database recovery, it is often extremely valuable to have recent backups of your control file and server parameter file. RMAN has the capability to enable control file and server parameter file autobackups. The autobackup occurs independently of any explicit backup of the current control file requested as part of your BACKUP command. If a control file autobackup is available, RMAN can recover the database even if the current control file, recovery catalog, and server parameter file are inaccessible. RMAN can also search for and restore the server parameter file from that autobackup. Once the instance has been started with the restored server parameter file, RMAN can restore the control file from the autobackup.

If the control file autobackup option is on, then RMAN will automatically back up the control file and the current server parameter file at the end of a successful BACKUP command. For databases running in ARCHIVELOG mode, RMAN will make a control file autobackup any time a structural change affects the contents of the control file. You can enable the autobackup feature by running the following command in RMAN:

```
CONFIGURE CONTROLFILE AUTOBACKUP ON;
```

You can disable it by running the following command:

```
CONFIGURE CONTROLFILE AUTOBACKUP OFF;
```

Scripting RMAN Backups

You can use RMAN command files to manage recurring tasks such as periodic backups. An RMAN command file is a client-side text file that contains RMAN commands. The commands in the file are formatted exactly as they are entered at the RMAN prompt. The RMAN command file can be given any file extension. The RUN command provides a degree of flow-of-control in your scripts. A basic command file might have a name like rman_command_file.txt and contain the following contents:

```
CONNECT TARGET /
BACKUP DATABASE PLUS ARCHIVELOG;
LIST BACKUP;
EXIT;
```

Once a command file exists, you can launch RMAN and simultaneously provide a command file to run. After the command completes, RMAN exits.

```
% rman @/tmp/rman_command_file.txt
```

Alternately, you can start RMAN and execute the contents of the file by using the @ command at the RMAN prompt:

```
% rman
RMAN> @/tmp/rman_command_file.txt
```

After the command file contents have been executed, RMAN displays the message "**end-of-file**". Unlike executing a command file from the operating system command line, RMAN does not exit after all commands complete.

It is possible to specify one or more values in a USING clause for use as substitution variables in a command file. With these, it is possible to make command files more dynamic. The syntax is identical to SQL*Plus, where &1 indicates the first value, &2 the second value, and so on. The specific syntax is &integer followed by an optional period. The optional period is part of the variable and is replaced with the substituted value. Substitution variables make it possible to use command files with a dynamic shell script. The script can then use an operating system scheduler like cron to automate the backup process.

The following example shows the contents of a command file named weekly_backup.cmd, which is run each week. The script uses substitution variables for three items:

- The name of the tape set.
- A portion of the string in the FORMAT specification.
- The name of the restore point to be created.

```
# weekly_backup.cmd
CONNECT TARGET /
RUN
{
ALLOCATE CHANNEL c1
DEVICE TYPE sbt
PARMS 'ENV=(OB_MEDIA_FAMILY=&1)';
BACKUP DATABASE
TAG &2
FORMAT '/u02/bck/&2%U.bck'
KEEP FOREVER
RESTORE POINT &3;
}
EXIT;
```

Enterprise Manager

You can also schedule backups through Oracle Enterprise Manager. You can access the Schedule Backup screen by selecting Availability from Enterprise Manager and then Schedule backup. From this screen, you can enable the Oracle-Suggested backup strategy or build a custom strategy of your own. The suggested strategy makes a one-time whole-database backup (incremental level-0). It then schedules incremental level-1 backups daily. Starting with day three onward, Oracle applies the level-1 backup from day n-1 to the level 0 backup before creating the current incremental backup for the day. You can instead create a customized backup and have a wide range of options to choose from in creating a backup strategy.

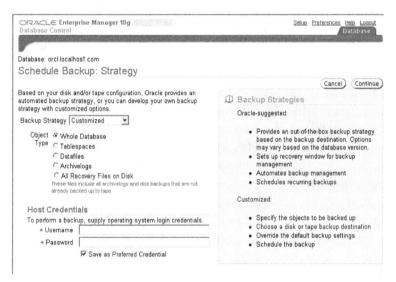

Manage backups, view backup reports and monitor the fast recovery area

The activities in this section are primarily performed via Oracle Enterprise Manager. In the exams where I've encountered questions on OEM, there's generally an exhibit with a screenshot of EM and a question regarding one element on the screen. This guide will detail the functionality of the EM screens, but ideally you should open Enterprise

Manager on your own and become familiar with the screens in order to be prepared for EM questions on the test.

Managing Backups

From Enterprise manager, select Availability and Manage Current Backup to access the 'Manage Current backups' screen. The information on this page includes:

- The date and time a backup completed.
- Where the backup was created.
- The contents of the backup.
- Whether it is still available.

You can also perform several backup functions from this page. At the top of the screen are four buttons that allow you to perform the following tasks:

- **Catalog Additional Files** – You can add backup files created by some means other than RMAN to the catalog.
- **Crosscheck All** – If files have been deleted using OS utilities, RMAN is unaware the files no longer exist. The crosscheck operation verifies what files truly exist on disk.
- **Delete All Obsolete** – This deletes any backups older that the retention policy.
- **Delete All Expired** – This removes the entry in the catalog for any backups found to be missing during a crosscheck.

Viewing Backup Reports

From Enterprise Manager, select Availability and then Backup Reports to access the Backup Reports screen. This page provides information from the control file for specific jobs. Some of the information available includes:

- Backup Name
- Status
- Start Time
- Duration
- Type

- Output Device
- Input and Output Sizes

Monitoring the Fast Recovery Area through SQL

The V$RECOVERY_FILE_DEST dynamic view displays information about the disk quota and current disk usage in the fast recovery area.

```
SELECT TRUNC(space_limit / (1024*1024)) "Limit (MB)",
       TRUNC(space_used / (1024*1024)) "Used (MB)",
       TRUNC(space_reclaimable / (1024*1024)) "Recl (MB)"
       number_of_files "# of files"
FROM   v$recovery_file_dest;

Limit (MB) Used (MB) Recl (MB) # of files
---------- --------- --------- ----------
      1000       644       390         20
```

You can determine additional information about the files taking up space in the fast recovery area from the V$RECOVERY_AREA_USAGE view. This view was called V$FLASH_RECOVERY_AREA_USAGE prior to 11.2 and may appear that way on the test. The view contains file type, percent of FRA space used, percent of FRA space that is reclaimable, and the number of files of that type.

```
SELECT file_type,
       percent_space_used AS SPACE_USED,
       percent_space_reclaimable AS RECLAIMABLE,
       number_of_files
FROM   v$recovery_area_usage;

FILE_TYPE     SPACE_USED RECLAIMABLE NUMBER_OF_FILES
---------     ---------- ----------- ---------------
CONTROLFILE            0           0               0
ONLINELOG              0           0               0
ARCHIVELOG         12.31        9.42              14
BACKUPPIECE        53.12       30.21               6
IMAGECOPY              0           0               0
FLASHBACKLOG           0           0               0
```

Monitoring the Fast Recovery Area through Enterprise Manager

From Enterprise manager, if you select Availability and then Recovery Settings, you will be in the Fast Recovery screen. From this page, you can perform the following tasks:

- Determine how much of the Fast Recovery Area has been used.
- Set the size of the Fast Recovery Area.
- Set the location of the Fast Recovery Area.
- Specify the Retention time.
- Configure Flashback Database.

Performing Database Recovery

Overview of Data Recovery Advisor

Functions of the DRA

Oracle's Data Recovery Advisor is a data corruption repair function integrated with Support Workbench, database health checks and RMAN. It can display data corruption problems, assess their extent and impact, recommend repair options, and automate the repair process. In the context of Data Recovery Advisor, a health check is a diagnostic procedure run by the Health Monitor to assess the state of the database or its components. Health checks are invoked reactively when an error occurs and can also be invoked manually.

Failures

A failure is a persistent data corruption detected by a health check. They are usually detected reactively when a database operation encounters corrupted data and generates an error. This will automatically invoke a health check in the database. The check will search the database for failures related to the error and record any findings in the Automatic Diagnostic Repository. Data Recovery Advisor can generate repair advice and repair failures only after failures have been detected by the database and stored in the ADR. Data Recovery Advisor can report on and repair failures such as inaccessible files, physical and logical block corruptions, and I/O failures. All failures are assigned a priority: CRITICAL, HIGH, or LOW, and a status of OPEN or CLOSED.

- **CRITICAL** priority failures require immediate attention because they make the whole database unavailable. Typically, critical failures bring down the instance and are diagnosed during the subsequent startup.
- **HIGH** priority failures make a database partially unavailable or unrecoverable, and usually have to be repaired in a reasonably short time.
- **LOW** priority indicates that failures can be ignored until more important failures are fixed.

Use Data Recovery Advisor to Perform Recovery

DRA Repairs

Data Recovery Advisor allows you to view repair options. Repairs might involve the use of block media recovery, datafile media recovery, or Oracle Flashback Database. In general, Data Recovery Advisor presents both automated and manual repair options. If appropriate, you can choose an automated repair option in order to perform a repair. In an automated repair, Data Recovery Advisor performs the repair, verifies the repair success, and closes the relevant failures.

The recommended workflow for repairing data failures from RMAN is to run the following commands in sequence during an RMAN session: LIST FAILURE to display failures, ADVISE FAILURE to display repair options, and REPAIR FAILURE to fix the failures.

LIST FAILURE

The LIST FAILURE command displays failures against which you can run the ADVISE FAILURE and REPAIR FAILURE commands.

```
RMAN> LIST FAILURE;
List of Database Failures
=============================
Failure ID Priority Status  Time Detected Summary
------ ---- ---- -------- ----
274          HIGH     OPEN     12-APR-11     One or more non-
system
                                             datafiles are
missing
329          HIGH     OPEN     12-APR-11     Datafile 1:

'/u01/oradata/prod/system01.dbf'
                                             contains one or
more corrupt blocks
```

ADVISE FAILURE

Use the ADVISE FAILURE command to display repair options for the specified failures. This command prints a summary of the failures identified by the Data Recovery Advisor and implicitly closes all open failures that are already fixed. The ADVISE FAILURE command indicates the repair strategy that Data Recovery Advisor considers optimal for a given set of failures. Data Recovery Advisor verifies repair feasibility before proposing a repair strategy. For example, it will check that all backups and archived redo log files needed for media recovery are available. It can generate both manual and automated repair options.

The ADVISE command maps a set of failures to the set of repair steps that Data Recovery Advisor considers to be optimal. When possible, Data Recovery Advisor consolidates multiple repair steps into a single repair. For example, if the database has corrupted datafile, missing control file, and lost current redo log group, then Data Recovery Advisor would recommend a single, consolidated repair plan to restore the database and perform point-in-time recovery.

```
RMAN> ADVISE FAILURE;
List of Database Failures
=========================
Failure Priority Status Time      Summary
------- -------- ------ --------- --------------------
274     HIGH     OPEN   12-APR-11 One or more non-system
                                  datafiles are missing
329     HIGH     OPEN   12-APR-11 Datafile 1:
                                  '/u01/oradata/prod/
                                  system01.dbf'
                                  contains one or more
                                  corrupt blocks

analyzing automatic repair options; this may take some time
using channel ORA_DISK_1
analyzing automatic repair options complete

Mandatory Manual Actions
========================
no manual actions available

Optional Manual Actions
=======================
1. If file /u01/oradata/prod/data01.dbf was unintentionally
renamed or moved, restore it

Automated Repair Options
========================
Option Repair Description
--- ---------
    1    Restore and recover datafile 31; Perform block
         media recovery of block 43481 in file 1
```

```
Strategy: The repair includes complete media recovery with no
data loss
Repair script:
/u01/oracle/log/diag/rdbms/prod/prod/hm/reco_740113269.hm
```

CHANGE FAILURE

The CHANGE FAILURE command allows you to change the failure priority from HIGH to LOW or the reverse, or to close it. You cannot change to or from CRITICAL priority.

```
RMAN> CHANGE FAILURE 3 PRIORITY LOW;
```

REPAIR FAILURE

The REPAIR FAILURE command is used to repair database failures identified by the Data Recovery Advisor. The target database instance must be started, it must be a single-instance database and cannot be a physical standby database. It is important that at most one RMAN session is running the REPAIR FAILURE command. The only exception is REPAIR FAILURE ... PREVIEW, which is permitted in concurrent RMAN sessions. To perform an automated repair, the Data Recovery Advisor may require specific backups and archived redo logs. If the files are not available, then the recovery will not be possible. Data Recovery Advisor consolidates repairs whenever possible so that a single repair can fix multiple failures. If one has not yet been issued in the current RMAN session, REPAIR FAILURE performs an implicit ADVISE FAILURE. RMAN always verifies that failures are still relevant and automatically closes failures that have already been repaired. After executing a repair, RMAN reevaluates all open failures on the chance that some of them may also have been fixed.

Moving Data

Describe and use methods to move data (Directory objects, SQL*Loader, External Tables)

Directory Objects

A directory object is a database object that acts as an alias for a directory on the server file system. Directory objects are used to define locations where external binary file LOBs (BFILEs) and external table data are located. They are also required for Data Pump operations. Directory objects are created in a single namespace and are not owned by an individual schema. Once created, users must be granted READ and/or WRITE access in order to be able to read or write from the location specified by the directory object.

```
CREATE DIRECTORY ocp_dir AS '/home/oracle/extfiles';
GRANT READ ON DIRECTORY ocp_dir TO ocpguru;
GRANT WRITE ON DIRECTORY ocp_dir TO ocpguru;
```

SQL*Loader

The SQL*Loader utility allows you to load data from external flat files into Oracle database tables. The parsing engine of SQL*Loader is very versatile and puts few limitations on the format of the data in the external file. SQL*Loader recognizes the data in the data file as records whether it is in fixed record format, variable record format, or stream record format. The record format is normally specified in the control file using the INFILE parameter. If no record format is specified, then the default is stream record format. SQL*Loader can perform the following tasks:

- Load data from multiple data files in a single load session.
- Load data into multiple tables in a single load session.
- Load data from different character sets.
- Load only selected data from a file.
- Load data across a network.
- Use SQL functions to transform the data before loading it.
- Generate unique sequential key values while loading.
- Use the operating system's file system to access the data files.
- Load data from disk, tape, or named pipe.

- Generate error reports to aid troubleshooting.
- Load complex object-relational data.
- Use secondary data files for loading LOBs and collections.

SQL*Loader sessions make use of the following files:
- **Control** – Defines the format of the data file and controls the behavior of SQL*Loader.
- **Data** – One or more data files will contain the information to be loaded.
- **Log** – Contains a log of the actions performed by SQL*Loader and errors encountered.
- **Bad** – Contains all records that could not be loaded due to errors.
- **Discard** – Contains all records that the control file identified to be bypassed.

The sqlldr executable is used to invoke SQL*Loader. It is optionally followed by parameters that establish session characteristics. Parameters can also be specified using the following methods instead of the command line:

- Parameters can be added to a parameter file. To use a parameter file, the name of the file can be supplied in the command line using the PARFILE parameter.
- Some parameters can be specified within the SQL*Loader control file using the OPTIONS clause.

If the same parameter is specified on the command line and in a parameter file or OPTIONS clause, the value in the command line is used.

The SQL*Loader control file is a text file that tells SQL*Loader where to find the data file, the format to use in parsing the data, what table(s) to insert the data in to, and more. A control file has three loosely-defined sections:

- The first section contains session-wide information such as global options, the input data file location, and the data to be loaded.

- The second section consists of one or more INTO TABLE blocks. The blocks hold information about the destination table.
- The third section is optional and, if present, contains input data.

SQL*Loader has two methods of inserting data into Oracle tables, Conventional Path and Direct Load options. In conventional path, SQL*Loader effectively creates INSERT statements for the records in the file to be loaded and passes them to the Oracle SQL Parser to be handled. When using Direct Path, SQL*Loader bypasses SQL and the parser and loads data directly into the target table(s). Direct Path load is much faster, but Conventional Path is more flexible. Some restrictions of the Direct Path load are:

- It cannot run concurrently with other transactions against the target table.
- Triggers on the table do not fire..
- Data is written above the high-water mark of the table even if there is space below.
- Clustered tables are not supported.
- Foreign Key constraints are disabled during the load.

External Tables

External tables are defined as tables that do not reside in the database. It's possible to have tables in any format for which an access driver is provided. Inside the Oracle data dictionary is stored metadata describing an external table. With this metadata, Oracle provides SQL access to the external table as if it were a regular database table. It's possible to perform SELECT and JOIN operations, or create views or synonyms against external tables. It is not possible to perform DML operations or create indexes on external tables.

The metadata for external tables is created using the ORGANIZATION EXTERNAL clause of the CREATE TABLE statement. An external table definition acts as a view against the external data. An access driver is mechanism by which the external data is read. Oracle Database provides two access drivers for external tables: ORACLE_LOADER and

ORACLE_DATAPUMP. ORACLE_LOADER reads data from external files using the Oracle Loader technology using a subset of the control file syntax of the SQL*Loader utility. ORACLE_DATAPUMP allows you to read data from the database and insert it into an external table, and then reload it into an Oracle Database. Note that while ORACLE_DATAPUMP allows writing to external files, the functionality is not performed via DML statements. The ANALYZE statement is not supported for gathering statistics for external tables, but you can use the DBMS_STATS package. Virtual columns are not supported on external tables. For an external table, the DROP TABLE statement removes only metadata in the database. It has no effect on the actual data outside of the database.

You create external tables using the CREATE TABLE statement with an ORGANIZATION EXTERNAL clause. This statement creates only metadata in the data dictionary. The following example creates an external table using the ORACLE_LOADER access method.

```
CREATE TABLE phone_list_ext (
   employee_id        VARCHAR2(5),
   first_name         VARCHAR2(50),
   last_name          VARCHAR2(50),
   phone              VARCHAR2(20)
)
ORGANIZATION EXTERNAL (
   TYPE ORACLE_LOADER
   DEFAULT DIRECTORY ext_tables
   ACCESS PARAMETERS (
     RECORDS DELIMITED BY NEWLINE FIELDS TERMINATED BY ','
     MISSING FIELD VALUES ARE NULL
     (
        employee_id        CHAR(5),
        first_name         CHAR(50),
        last_name          CHAR(50),
        phone              CHAR(20)
     )
   )
   LOCATION ('phone_list.txt')
)
PARALLEL 2
REJECT LIMIT UNLIMITED;
```

The example above uses the ORACLE_LOADER access driver. This driver is used for reading text files. Essentially any file that SQL*Loader can read from can be used as an external table. The parameters in the ACCESS PARAMETERS clause are opaque to the database. These access parameters are specific to the access driver. Oracle provides these parameters to the access driver when the external table is accessed. The PARALLEL clause enables parallel query on the data sources. The REJECT LIMIT clause specifies that there is no limit on the number of errors that can occur during a query of the external data.

Only the following ALTER TABLE Clause options are allowed on external tables:

- **REJECT LIMIT** – Changes the reject limit.
- **PROJECT COLUMN REFERENCED** – The access driver processes only the columns in the select list of the query. This setting may not provide a consistent set of rows when querying a different column list from the same external table but can speed up access.
- **PROJECT COLUMN ALL** – The access driver processes all of the columns defined on the external table. This setting always provides a consistent set of rows when querying an external table. This is the default.
- **DEFAULT DIRECTORY** – Changes the default directory specification.

Explain the general architecture of Oracle Data Pump

Oracle Data Pump is designed to provide high-speed movement of data and metadata from one database to another. It replaces the export/import functionality that existed in earlier releases of Oracle. Data Pump is made up of three distinct parts:

- **expdp and impdp** – These are command-line clients that use the procedures provided in the DBMS_DATAPUMP package to execute export and import commands. They accept parameters entered at the command line that enable the exporting and importing of data and metadata for a complete database or for subsets of a database.

- **DBMS_DATAPUMP** – Also known as the Data Pump API, this package provides a high-speed mechanism to move all or part of the data and metadata for a site from one database to another. DBMS_DATAPUMP can be used independently of the impdp and expdp clients.
- **DBMS_METADATA** – Also known as the Metadata API, this package provides a centralized facility for the extraction, manipulation, and re-creation of dictionary metadata. DBMS_METADATA can be used independently of the impdp and expdp clients.

Data Pump jobs use a master table, a master process, and worker processes to perform the work and keep track of progress:

- **Master Table** – A master table is used to track the progress within a job while the data and metadata are being transferred. It is implemented as a user table within the database. A user performing an impdp or expdp must have the CREATE TABLE system privilege for the master table to be created plus sufficient tablespace quota. The master table will have the same name as the job that created it. A Data Pump job cannot have the same name as an existing table or view in that schema. The information in the master table is used to restart a job.
- **Master process** – A master process is created for every Data Pump Export job and Data Pump Import job. It controls the entire job, including communicating with the clients, creating and controlling a pool of worker processes, and performing logging operations.
- **Worker Process** – The master process allocates work to be executed to worker processes that perform the data and metadata processing within an operation. Data Pump can employ multiple worker processes, running in parallel, to increase job performance.

Monitor a Data Pump job

It's possible to use the Data Pump Export and Import utilities to attach to a running job. When attached in logging mode, status about the job is automatically displayed during execution in real-time. When attached using interactive-command mode, it's possible to request the job status.

Optionally, a log file can be written during the execution of a job. It summarizes the progress of the job, lists any errors, and records the completion status. You can also determine job status or to get other information about Data Pump jobs, through the Data Pump views:

- **DBA_DATAPUMP_JOBS** – Identifies all active Data Pump jobs in the database, regardless of their state, on an instance (or on all instances for RAC). It also shows all Data Pump master tables not currently associated with an active job.
- **DBA_DATAPUMP_SESSIONS** – Identifies the user sessions that are attached to a Data Pump job. The information in this view is useful for determining why a stopped Data Pump operation has not gone away.
- **V$SESSION_LONGOPS** – Data Pump operations that transfer table data (export and import) maintain an entry indicating the job progress. The entry contains the estimated transfer size and is periodically updated to reflect the actual amount of data transferred.

The V$SESSION_LONGOPS columns that are relevant to a Data Pump job are as follows:

- **USERNAME** - job owner
- **OPNAME** - job name
- **TARGET_DESC** - job operation
- **SOFAR** - megabytes transferred thus far during the job
- **TOTALWORK** - estimated number of megabytes in the job
- **UNITS** - megabytes (MB)
- **MESSAGE** - a formatted status message of the form: 'job_name: operation_name : nnn out of mmm MB done'

Use Data Pump Export and Import to move data between Oracle databases

The Data Pump Export utility is invoked using the expdp command. The actions performed by the export operation are defined by the parameters you specify. They can be supplied either on the command line or in a parameter file. Data Pump Export can be controlled using a command line, a parameter file, or an interactive-command mode:

- **Command-Line** – Enables you to specify most of the export parameters from the command line.
- **Parameter File** – Allows you to specify command-line parameters in a parameter file. The PARFILE parameter cannot be used in a parameter file, because parameter files cannot be nested.
- **Interactive-Command** – Displays an export prompt from which you can enter various commands. Some commands are specific to interactive-command mode.

Data Pump jobs manage the following types of files:

- **Dump files** – Contain the data and metadata being moved.
- **Log files** – Record the messages associated with an operation.
- **SQL files** – Record the output of a SQLFILE operation.
- **Data Files** – Files specified by the DATA_FILES parameter during a transportable import.

There are different expdp modes for unloading different portions of the database. The mode is specified using the appropriate parameter. The available modes are:

- **Full** – In a full database export, the entire database is unloaded. This mode requires the user performing the export to have the DATAPUMP_EXP_FULL_DATABASE role. Specified using the FULL parameter.
- **Schema** – This is the default export mode. If you have the DATAPUMP_EXP_FULL_DATABASE role, then you can provide a list of schemas to export. Otherwise you can export only your own schema. Specified using the SCHEMAS parameter.

- **Table** – In table mode, only a specified set of tables, partitions, and their dependent objects are unloaded. You must have the DATAPUMP_EXP_FULL_DATABASE role to export tables that are not in your own schema. Specified using the TABLES parameter.
- **Tablespace** – In tablespace mode, only the tables contained in a specified set of tablespaces are unloaded. If a table is unloaded, then its dependent objects are also unloaded. Privileged users get all tables. Unprivileged users get only the tables in their own schemas. Specified using the TABLESPACES parameter.
- **Transportable Tablespace** – In transportable tablespace mode, only the metadata for the tables (and their dependent objects) within a specified set of tablespaces is exported. The tablespace data files are copied in a separate operation. Specified using the TRANSPORT_TABLESPACES parameter.

expdp Parameters

The following parameters are applicable to expdp:

- **ATTACH** – Attaches the client session to an existing export job and automatically places you in the interactive-command interface.
- **CONTENT** – Enables you to filter what Export unloads: data only, metadata only, or both.
- **DIRECTORY** – Specifies the default location to which Export can write the dump file set and the log file.
- **DUMPFILE** – Specifies the names, and optionally, the directory objects of dump files for an export job.
- **ESTIMATE** – Specifies the method that Export will use to estimate how much disk space each table in the export job will consume (in bytes).
- **ESTIMATE_ONLY** – Instructs Export to estimate the space that a job would consume, without actually performing the export operation.
- **EXCLUDE** – Enables you to filter the metadata that is exported by specifying objects and object types to be excluded from the export operation.
- **FILESIZE** – Specifies the maximum size of each dump file.
- **FULL** – Specifies that you want to perform a full database mode export.

- **INCLUDE** – Enables you to filter the metadata that is exported by specifying objects and object types for the current export mode.
- **JOB_NAME** – Used to identify the export job in subsequent actions.
- **LOGFILE** – Specifies the name, and optionally, a directory, for the log file of the export job.
- **PARFILE** – Specifies the name of an export parameter file.
- **QUERY** – Allows you to specify a query clause that is used to filter the data that gets exported.
- **SCHEMAS** – Specifies that you want to perform a schema-mode export.
- **TABLES** – Specifies that you want to perform a table-mode export.
- **TABLESPACES** – Specifies a list of tablespace names to be exported in tablespace mode.

impdp Parameters

Many of the above parameters are also applicable to impdp. In addition, several of the more common impdp parameters are:

- **REUSE_DATAFILES** – Specifies whether the import job should reuse existing data files for tablespace creation.
- **SQLFILE** – Specifies a file into which all of the SQL DDL that Import would have executed, based on other parameters, is written.
- **STATUS** – Specifies the frequency at which the job status display is updated.
- **TABLE_EXISTS_ACTION** – Tells import what to do if the table it is trying to create already exists.
- **REMAP_DATAFILE** – Changes the name of the source data file to the target data file name in all SQL statements where the source data file is referenced.
- **REMAP_SCHEMA** – Loads all objects from the source schema into a target schema.
- **REMAP_TABLE** – Allows you to rename tables during an import operation.
- **REMAP_TABLESPACE** – Remaps all objects selected for import with persistent data in the source tablespace to be created in the target tablespace.

The following commands are applicable when using Interactive mode:

- **ADD_FILE** – Add additional dump files.
- **CONTINUE_CLIENT** – Exit interactive mode and enter logging mode.
- **EXIT_CLIENT** – Stop the import or export client session, but leave the job running.
- **KILL_JOB** – Detach all currently attached client sessions and terminate the current job.
- **PARALLEL** – Increase or decrease the number of active worker processes for the current job.
- **START_JOB** – Restart a stopped job to which you are attached.
- **STATUS** – Display detailed status for the current job and/or set status interval.
- **STOP_JOB** – Stop the current job for later restart.

ABOUT THE AUTHOR

Matthew Morris is an Oracle Database Administrator and Developer currently employed as a Database Engineer with Computer Sciences Corporation. Matthew has worked with the Oracle database since 1996 when he worked in the RDBMS support team for Oracle Support Services. Employed with Oracle for over eleven years in support and development positions, Matthew was an early adopter of the Oracle Certified Professional program. He was one of the first one hundred Oracle Certified Database Administrators (version 7.3) and in the first hundred to become an Oracle Certified Forms Developer. In the years since, he has upgraded his Database Administrator certification for releases 8i, 9i, 10G and 11G, , become an Oracle Advanced PL/SQL Developer Certified Professional and added the Application Express and SQL Expert certifications. Outside of Oracle, he has CompTIA certifications in Linux+ and Security+.

www.ingramcontent.com/pod-product-compliance
Lightning Source LLC
Chambersburg PA
CBHW071202050326
40689CB00011B/2217